"Pennie Saum's memoir is an overwhelmingly powerful and honest retelling of a horrific tormented childhood. She steps out of the silence that comes with childhood sexual abuse and brings forward the reality of the impact of trauma such as this. She has intertwined her childhood past with her mother's battle and how the two stories relate. Brave and Unbroken is a perfect title for Pennie's story. Her ability to share her voice, overcome horrific trauma and help make change for others is a true testament of her bravery and a story that everyone should read."

-**Marilyn Van Derbur,** author of *Miss America By Day.*
www.MissAmericaByDay.com

"Pennie Saum grew up on military bases around the world, but no matter where she lived, the scenario was unchanged: grounded in a foundation of maternal love, laughter, and goodness, juxtaposed with paternal manipulation, hatred, and never-ending sexual abuse. Pennie gives us the gift of stepping into her courageous, decades-long fight for survival and following along as she finds blessings beneath the pain. It is a life-changing read."

-**Kathleen Prezbindowski, Ph.D., M.S.N.**
Biologist and long-term wellness/support group Facilitator

"Pennie Saum's heroic story of surviving sexual abuse could not have arrived at a more appropriate time in our nation's history. The patchwork of raw memories Pennie shares unabashedly fills the pages in Brave and Unbroken - and will undoubtedly save lives for the sheer essence of being told. Her story should be read by young and old, gay and straight, survivors and therapists - humans everywhere."

-**Sarah Toce,**
Award-winning journalist and publisher

BRAVE
and
unbroken

The true story of survival after incest and loss.

Pennie Saum

with Cat Caperello

Brave and Unbroken
A True Story of Survival After Incest and Loss
Copyright 2018 by Pennie Saum

Address inquiries to:

Pennie Saum
PO BOX 952
Puyallup, WA 98371

info@penniesaum.com
www.braveandunbroken.com

Paperback Cover ISBN: 978-1-54393-089-4
eBook ISBN: 978-1-54393-090-0
Library of Congress Control Number: 2018904996

Editor: Kathy Prezbendowski
Cover layout: Lisa Snyder
Cover concept: Pennie Saum
Interior design and layout: BookBaby

Every attempt has been made to source properly all quotes.
Printed in the United States of America

For additional copies visit: www.braveandunbroken.com

I dedicate this book to my younger self.

When no one knew, you were strong.
When no one saw, you were brave.
You are a warrior – Brave and Unbroken, never forget it.

Always choose truth, always choose you. xoxo

To each of you who have ever suffered childhood sexual abuse, please know:

YOU are seen.

YOU are heard.

YOU Matter.

YOU can move from victim to survivor to thriver.

YOU are not alone.

xo Pennie

www.braveandunbroken.com

Contents

Chapter 1: These Old Walls   1

Chapter 2: Miss Debby   6

Chapter 3: An Officer and a Predator   22

Chapter 4: Treatment   26

Chapter 5: Saving Grace   31

Chapter 6: Going Home   46

Chapter 7: Crimes and Punishment   69

Chapter 8: I'll Fly Away   86

Chapter 9: Tear Down the Walls   104

Chapter 10: Be the Change   132

Acknowledgements   160

CHAPTER 1

These Old Walls

"There's Ama's house."

"Ama" is the endearing term that my oldest gave my mother when he was young and couldn't say "grandma." She always said that the boys would give her a name.

Tyler's voice catches me off guard. I hadn't noticed we would drive by her house. This was the first time in quite a while. I had forgotten about it in a few turns, when my youngest son spoke up from the passenger seat. His words are wistful, but his brow furrows with the emotions stirring inside him. I can see it on his face, and I can't blame him.

"I wish we could have kept it," he said.

I know that he's frustrated we sold the house, and that not having it in our family anymore has been hard on him. He just doesn't understand yet. In his mind, his grandmother's home brought him great joy, but I keep thinking of the holes in the bathroom door.

"Tyler, that house holds a lot of great memories for you and your brother with Ama, but that house holds a lot of really bad memories for me. At some point in your life, when you're older, you'll realize what some of those bad memories are and what their impact has been."

Not much has changed on the outside of the yellow rambler since we were all there together: his Ama, his older brother Jaycob, and I. A lot of my mother's stone figures were still where she placed them around the yard. A strange car is in the driveway, sure, but really, the whole thing felt different. Her spirit was missing.

I think about how confusing this is for him and think back to a slumber party my two sons and I had on my mother's living room floor after the house was empty, but before it had sold. While they are making new memories, so many of my old memories rush in.

This must feel unfair to him.

"Tyler, as much as I would have loved to keep that house for you, that's just not something I could do and feel good about."

We nicknamed my mother's house the "dollhouse." Each wall was painted a different color, and some had both paint and wallpaper. She had mementos and trinkets everywhere, covering the walls, in the cabinets, on the shelves, and each item had a story. A glass knick-knack shelf was filled with the Swarovski crystal animals she loved: swans, teddy bears, and other creatures. We sought out new crystal creatures every holiday as special gifts for her. Paint-by-number artwork that we made for her one Mother's Day had hung in the hall over the telephone stand. Handmade ceramics of a sailor with a pipe in his mouth, a farmer with a straw hat, and Elvis, all from Germany hung on the walls. The Italian ceramics were my mother's favorite, though. She bought them on vacation directly from the factory in Venezia where they were made. They were fancy porcelain creations with intricate, handmade flowers, petals, and leaves. Every time I saw them, they reminded me of a bizarre family trip we took to Italy. We had one of those Dodge Ram vans and drove it from Germany to a city outside of Venice. This was a square van, with seats and table in the back, a luggage rack on top, and painted two shades of brown.

The second morning of the trip we stayed at a bed and breakfast in Venezia. Don, my biological father, told us that our van had been broken into, and several of the ceramics, among other things, were stolen. My brother and I were itching to get outside and explore, but Don made us stay inside the bed and breakfast on lockdown while he kept disappearing. He said that he had to go to Italian court regarding the theft. The story was long and convoluted. He'd come back, and to pass the time on lockdown, he played photographer. As usual, he made me wear particular pieces of clothing, such as a low-cut top, and made me strike certain poses for the camera. I was present physically, but not mentally.

Over the years, during fits of rage, Don broke the few Italian ceramics that hadn't been "stolen." My mom would glue them back together, time after time. When he moved out, I tried to get her to box them up, but she wouldn't let them go. I suppose each of them had meaning for her. She had saved up money for over a year to afford these specific collectable souvenirs while we in Italy. Each porcelain flower, each basket she selected, and they all meant something. She always seemed to overlook the bad memories that each piece carried and only recall where and how each had been acquired.

Our family lived in the yellow rambler for twenty-six years, and many things happened in that house. If those walls could talk, they would tell tales of terror, fear, hate, and survival. Memories that could never be washed away with the incarceration of the terrible man I knew as my biological father. Memories that even the sounds of my children's laughter, so many years later, couldn't erase.

My mother fought hard for us kids. She loved us enough that even after years of enduring abuse, she tried to change this place into a safe space and into her own temple after he went away. She dug deep into her soul and made this house a place of safety and love. She changed our story, she reversed our fear, and renewed our lives. If the walls could talk, they would tell of our resilience, of new stories casting out the old. Magical Christmases, turkey feasts with all the trimmings, and family gatherings; the joys of new grandchildren, and how things began to seem normal for the first time; movie nights and popcorn; enchiladas and extended stays; and all the treats grandchildren could imagine. My mother loved my two sons, her only grandchildren. She called them her angels. Other adults and family members were ordered to stay away when it was Ama time so that there were no rules for the boys, only fun. The walls will tell of love, laughter, silliness, and all three, Ama and the two boys, up chewing gum clear until the sunrise the next morning. My sons were lucky. I wondered if she was making up for lost time.

My mother celebrated our family with pictures everywhere. My graduation portrait, my boys' school pictures, my brother, my grandparents, and my aunt and her family. My mother loved having family photos, and she made sure that everyone was represented. Almost everyone. The house is a small three-bedroom rambler, and the largest bedroom at the back of the house was my mother's bedroom. She had a brand-new four-poster oak bed, and she was so proud of it. She saved her money and paid cash for it. That was a big deal to her, to have done that for herself: to buy new nice things.

The walls showcase awards that my mother had received over the years from her job at the military clothing store on the Army base. My mother, Debby, took great pride in her home: new carpets, fresh paint. She would spend hours outside, weeding, planting, and mowing. The yard always looked great and inviting. Her home was her castle. That's what Tyler remembers, but my mind keeps going back to the peep holes in the bathroom door.

CHAPTER 2

Miss Debby

"Maybe it was the asbestos."

I can remember my mother mentioning for years she worked in buildings with asbestos and saying that if she ever got sick, I should go after the Army. She started with Army and Air Force Exchange Service (AAFES) when we went to Germany in 1984. AAFES is a for-profit company that supports the bases with supplies. AAFES services run the gamut, from food vending to uniforms and military clothing. Prior to this she worked at McDonald's while we lived in Maryland, where I attended elementary school. She worked during the hours that I was in school and was home from work by the time I got home from school. AAFES was a step up for her, but no matter what, she was in it for the people. My mother loved people and made friends quickly.

Later, when we got to Fort Lewis, outside Seattle, Washington in 1988, she worked on base. She got a job in the military clothing store that supplied all the badges, patches, and dress uniforms. My mother was always a natural with customer service, and she quickly became an expert on military uniforms. Each summer Fort Lewis hosted a Reserve Officer Training Corps (ROTC) camp, and my mother was put in charge of their military clothing. She would see the same soldiers year after year. Military bases make fast family, and she really got to know these kids. Some called her "mom," others called her "Miss Debby." It was sweet.

She was promoted to supervisor at military clothing, and her team loved her. She spoke highly of how everyone got their work done and kept their areas clean. Everyone always seemed to have fun with my mom. She was so proud of this job, her work, her staff, and her customers. Later they told me stories like when it was closing time at the liquor store, she would lay on the counter, a mock party animal, while they were cleaning up. She was just the type of person whose team had fun, but always got the work done. She had high expectations but exercised her authority in a loving way. One young man, a laborer who moved boxes of stock, was developmentally disabled, and my mother just kept giving him chance after chance to help him be productive and ways to feel valued as exactly who he was in the world.

During the summer ROTC camps, Miss Debby's heart strings got pulled on quite a bit. A lot of the participants were away from home for the first time, and they were right out of high school and headed into college. Some looked like deer in headlights. She would go running around after hours to other stores to get things they requested, whether it be a certain flavor of Gatorade or stamps so that they could mail letters home. Sometimes they would just give letters to her, and she would mail them.

"They're just boys." She would say, "They need care. They need to be loved!" She would go over and above to try to get everybody what they needed. My mother cared for those boys as if they were her own. She enjoyed a wonderful career at Fort Lewis from 1989 until 2011, three or four years before she got sick. She always blamed that summer store for her cancer: the old military barracks on Fort Lewis where they would set up the ROTC camp. Every year the store would be set up in the same building.

"If I ever get any kind of cancer, you have them check for asbestos," she insisted. I've thought about it, but I don't have any clue what I would have done. She mentioned the asbestos in that building multiple times. But I had bigger battles to fight against demons that were in my very bed. I didn't have the energy to think about protesting asbestos at Fort Lewis.

That was the thing about my mother: no matter how much abuse she endured in her life with my biological father, somehow, she still managed to have enough love to give to others. I don't know how she did it. She was like a fountain, endlessly flowing, sharing love with the world through her smile and her care. If only we could all have such a wellspring of beautiful energy.

• • •

My mom found the lumps on her neck on an unseasonably cool spring afternoon.

I remember it was a Sunday in early June. My mother came to drop something off, and immediately I knew something wasn't right. She looked drained. All the energy gone from her face, and she was complaining of an ache in her neck. Debby never complained about anything and I've seen her in some awful places. "I don't know, I think I slept wrong," she said, massaging this puffy, swollen area with these two lumps on the left side of her neck. The lumps were hard as pebbles. Her neck was stiff and sore. I noticed it immediately. She wanted my opinion about whether she should go to the clinic.

"I don't know what happened," my mom said, standing in my kitchen, "this came out of nowhere. I don't understand it."

The truth is that my mom was also not super tuned into her body. Whatever signs may have manifested, and I would be shocked if signs hadn't shown up prior to this, knowing her, she would just have ignored. Chalk it up to a bad day or depression.

"I just woke up and there they were," she repeated.

There they were, indeed. I looked at her, trying to mask my immediate concern, the thought of lymph nodes. They're famous for swelling, and can get stiff and painful when a person isn't feeling well. But these lumps weren't in the right place. My mother's lumps were on the outside of her neck, not toward the front. It just didn't add up, and I was immediately concerned.

"I probably just slept funny," she said again, but my mother's eyes betrayed the truth. I saw fear in them, and she agreed to go the urgent care clinic right away, that same day. I just looked at her for a moment in my kitchen and took it all in. I could feel something shift in me and our relationship. Something moved me to photograph my mother that day. This wasn't unusual, really. *I constantly take pictures of everything and everyone*, I told myself, reasoning over a growing discomfort. By the time she left to go to the clinic, I had already begun thinking that something was terribly wrong. I knew it in my gut, but I couldn't burden my mother with my premonitions. I knew she was staring down the barrel of her own journey.

The house was bustling with people. After my mother left, I looked over and said to a friend sitting at my kitchen table: "This isn't good," I said, "something doesn't feel right." My heart sank into the pit of my stomach and started to ache as the wait began.

The clinicians at urgent care gave her some medication for the pain and sent her to her primary care doctor for imaging. The next day she received a call that they wanted to biopsy the areas that were bothering her. They hadn't seen anything like it, they said, and they wanted to do some tests to understand what was going on. By Friday of the same week, only four days after I'd snapped the photo on that cool Sunday afternoon, she had been to three appointments and had two scans and a biopsy. She went on her own to the follow-up appointment with the oncologist. Everyone in the family received a group text message: "This is a shock. I have a lung cancer."

I immediately received a follow-up text directly to me: "I am scared. I have too much to live for."

Lung cancer echoed in my head.

I went with her to the next oncology appointment. The oncologist ordered more tests to better understand what type of cancer we were dealing with and identify the best treatment plan. Her next appointment was scheduled during a week that I needed to be out-of-state for a work conference. I hated not being with her to hear things for myself and ask questions.

My mother's sister, Barbara, flew up from Texas. She and my grandmother accompanied my mom to that next oncology appointment. The doctor explained that my mother's cancer was small cell lung cancer. My grandmother and mother insisted they heard the doctor say, "I can cure this cancer." Later my aunt clarified that she heard him say it was treatable, not curable. This was an important moment, I wish I had been present to hear it for myself. That night mom called to tell me how the appointment went. I sat in a hotel room in Indianapolis and wept.

Debby had smoked from age sixteen. When I was young she smoked Parliaments, and she switched over to generic cigarettes in Germany and whenever money was tight. She smoked in the house until my boys were born, then she smoked in the garage. She never smoked in the car when the boys were around. During tough times she would smoke one after the other. I've seen her chain smoke like you wouldn't believe, but on vacation with my boys, she cut back to as few as two or three cigarettes a day.

I always hated her smoking. You hear stories about people like George Burns who smoked like a chimney, drank a fifth of liquor, and lived to be one hundred. The reality is that smoking is smoking, and some people get lung cancer and others don't. Watching my mother have cancer was hard, especially since it was self-inflicted.

My aunt was also a smoker. I don't know when she started, but, along with my mother, she had smoked as long as I could remember. Also like my mother, she had tried to quit multiple times. My grandmother always dismissed my mom's smoking because smoking was the one outlet she had to deal with the stress through all the horrible times. I understood that, but I had conversations with my mom about quitting. I begged her for years to quit smoking cigarettes.

Don, my biological father, was a smoker too, but very inconsiderate. He didn't care who he smoked around. He didn't care about the mess he made, dropping ashes everywhere or stinky overflowing ashtrays. To be clear, he was an asshole about smoking. He would blow smoke in people's faces and use his smoking as a way to control and make others miserable. I remember when we would be driving together as a family, and he smoked so that the whole car would be filled with smoke, but we weren't allowed to so much as crack a window.

When he was out of the picture, I remember saying, "Mom, I hope you can quit smoking so you can stay with me for a really long time." I was already down one parent; I couldn't stand the thought of losing her as well. I even remember telling her I wanted her to take vitamins.

As a mother myself, I've always thought about who would take care of my boys if something happened to me. I wanted it to be my mom, but the smoking was a problem even though she didn't do it around them. I was always worried about the long-term effects on her health. I even tried to use guardianship for the boys to encourage her to finally stop for good. I asked if she would be the godmother for my sons. I told her I wanted her to have the boys and be responsible for their care if something happened to me. I hoped it would help motivate her to quit smoking cigarettes so that she could be around for a long time to be a pillar of stability for them.

She bristled and said she would try to quit, but she couldn't promise anything. She would have been by far the best person to take care of them, and even though not every smoker gets lung cancer, I knew the odds and couldn't make that choice for Jaycob and Tyler. We never talked about it again.

And there it was: my mother had been diagnosed with lung cancer, and finally, after all these years, she quit smoking cold turkey.

No struggle. No fighting. It's amazing how sometimes the unthinkable can bring out a person's strength. Quitting wasn't easy, but she did it. She kept saying she had everything to live for. I wish she could have seen that back in 2000 when she visited the primary care doctor she had been seeing since we moved to Washington. He told her that her lungs were in "great shape." She used that as justification and fuel for her case to continue to smoke even as I asked her to quit. June 2014 that same physician told her that she had lung cancer. I can't help but hate that.

She quit smoking and drinking International House of Coffee Cafe Francais and Mt. Dew on the same day. She had to. They were part of her ritual. Every morning she got up, peeled open the can of Cafe Francais, made her cup, added a big scoop of honey then she went out on the front porch or in the garage, cup steaming. In the garage, she had her smoke and her coffee and started her day. Later, when on breaks at work, it was Mt. Dew, with lots of ice in a plastic cup, and her smoke. These things just went hand in hand. She couldn't see having one without the other. For her, they all went together.

Cigarettes, powdered coffee with honey, and soda pop. She quit all that within the first week of her diagnosis. Thinking back on it now, I can't believe she didn't go into shock. I don't know how people quit things cold turkey. Part of me was proud of her, but part of me felt resentful she had taken so long to quit; it took this diagnosis for her to finally understand that it mattered.

I knew how many times over the years she had tried to quit and was unsuccessful. I knew quitting had been a battle for her, especially if she saw someone smoking or was around someone who was smoking. One time she was standing outside of a store and this guy drove up and asked for directions. He had a cigarette hanging out of his mouth, a yellowish cloud wafting from his open window. My mother was beside herself. She said that she had wanted to help him but wanted his cigarette so badly she couldn't think of anything else. So, I know quitting wasn't easy. She must've tried half a dozen times over the years.

What was odd to me was that my mom was so shocked she had lung cancer. Respectfully, she just couldn't get her head around how she'd gotten it and kept bringing up the asbestos. I'm sure it didn't help, but denial is powerful thing. One day I finally had enough. "Mom, it's the smoking," I said, keeping myself calm although I was seething. "How could it not be the smoking?" Of course, it was the smoking. I just couldn't believe that she was so surprised!

I was also upset because she was such a wonderful person. The saying that "bad things happen to good people" rings true here. My mom was dealt some hard cards. She had to overcome a lot of obstacles in her life, and I knew smoking was her outlet, was the one vice she allowed herself for being the victim of so much abuse and pain.

Unfortunately, some things you just can't outrun.

• • •

My grandmother had to grow up fast to cope with the experiences of her life. She tried to make her way through the world, hardened, but did her best. My great-grandmother had her at age sixteen, which was far from accepted at that time. A large enough age difference between my great-grandfather, an Army man, and my great-grandmother existed at the time that if they had been together today, their relationship would probably be illegal.

My great-grandmother was very much a man-pleaser. She didn't know how to function without a man. She would go from one husband to the next without a gap, pawning off her kids, pretending she didn't have any, and the next man would be none-the-wiser. My grandmother and her brother were raised by an aunt and a grandparent, on an "extended stay," as my grandmother called it. Her own mother was out courting men and didn't want them to know she had kids. That was her modus operandi.

My mom and my aunt always considered my great-grandmother a favorite grandmother because she was a wonderful grandmother; but she was just a terrible mother. After my great-grandmother's second husband died, within two or three weeks, my grandparents (her daughter and son-in-law) drove up to see her in New York. They brought her a new television. My grandmother must have hoped things were changing. Although my great-grandmother knew her daughter was traveling to see her, when my grandparents got to her home, she answered the door and said, "I've got Larry now, I don't need you anymore." She shut the door in their faces. My grandmother was devastated. In many ways she hadn't had a mother or father growing up, and while very set in her ways, I believe she truly tried to do the best she could.

My mom did a lot to make sure my grandmother was happy, and if my grandmother felt a certain way about something, my mom would change or shift, like a classic codependent. It wasn't until my mom's last few years that she spoke up a bit more, and wasn't as passive.

My grandmother was negative all the time. If you said you loved French fries, she would correct you and say that you *like* French fries and you *love* people. She liked attention. If two people went into another room to talk about something, she believed that they were gossiping about her. If a person was talking to my grandpa, then that person darn well better be talking to her as well, or she would get angry.

When my son Jaycob was still very young, we attended a family baby shower at which one of the shower games featured a bottle of lotion as the prize. Jaycob won, and my grandma insisted he hand over the lotion to me, as his mother, immediately.

"You're just a selfish little brat!" she chastised when he was reluctant. I didn't speak to her for three weeks after that, because I wanted to try to make her understand that she was the adult, and I wanted her to act like it. I loved her, but she was difficult. All a product of her upbringing.

My mom was born in Fort Brag, North Carolina to Army parents. My grandparents were transferred to Army bases, from North Carolina to Texas, and Oklahoma, before they were stationed overseas. My mom had only one sibling, Barbara who is four years younger. They have similar heights, vibrant red hair, and similar laughs and smiles. That's where similarities ended. Aesthetically, my mom liked to keep her hair long, but my aunt liked hers short.

My mother and her sister also had different points of view on how they handled themselves in the world. My mom was the type of person who would put a lot of forethought into her actions and how they might impact those around her. She was proud of telling stories in which she'd stopped to think about the consequences of her actions, what her mom would think, and the reactions of her parents. Then she would stop, not do whatever the questionable act was, and call for a ride home. My grandmother called her a saint. While my mother wasn't perfect and probably did something wrong, you'd be hard pressed to find someone who could point out specifics.

My Aunt Barbara was the wild child. Most of the time she would do whatever she wanted and deal with the consequences afterward. She had "learn-about-sex" books on her coffee table so that her daughter would be empowered to talk about sex, while my mom, would never mention the topic and deflected questions and discussion of the matter.

Despite the fact that both families were in the military, we were never stationed in the same place at the same time. But my mom and my Aunt B were on the telephone with each other constantly. They would talk through kid problems, what was going on at work, and everything, except hard stuff, like my parents' marriage.

When my mother said that she had too much to live for, my sons were big part of that equation for her. Jaycob was the first. I had a miscarriage a year to the day before I found out that I was pregnant with him. She was so upset at losing the chance to be a grandmother the previous year that I couldn't wait to share this news with her. I cut some notes out of a baby catalog and put them in a card for her to open. I remember driving to her house with the news. She always loved kids and animals. For her, babies were a fresh start. A new beginning. She was beside herself with excitement.

She was away visiting Aunt B when I found out about Tyler. I gave her the news over the telephone, and she was thrilled that her second grandson was coming and she would now get to have *two* angels.

My mother was the type of grandmother who most kids wish they had. She would take the boys to the coast for a week or spend the day taking them to garage sales. I wasn't invited to join them because my mother insisted grandma time meant no parent rules. She loved to make spaghetti with Ragu sauce the way they liked it or take them to El Toro, their favorite Mexican restaurant for chips and enchilada sauce, or "treat" them to their favorite Kid Cuisine frozen dinners.

One of my mother's special recipes was a version of goulash. True goulash from Germany is like a beef stew, and after living in Germany our family knows that, but my mom's recipe called for hamburger, tomato soup, and elbow macaroni. To this day my sons ask me to make "Ama Soup."

They watched movies and played games together. They went to Chuck E. Cheese's, and she would jump around in the ball pit with them for hours. We would laugh at how long my mom could last at a video pizza playground intended for children. She never hesitated to do anything with them. She took days off from work to spend time with the boys during summer vacation for a week, and on day nine she'd call me and tell me they were staying out for another day, and she'd call the next day and tell me they were staying out another day. She was the grandma that everyone wanted.

She was quirky too. My mom had dentures, and we always had such a time with them. Whenever she'd go somewhere for lunch, like McDonald's with the boys, she would take out one set, either the top or the bottom, because they hurt, and inevitably she would throw her teeth out with the tray. We would all be pawing through the garbage, trying to find her dentures. It was silly, but she always made light of it, and the boys laughed. I think her joviality with her grandchildren was pure relaxation, but also a way for her to counterbalance having been oppressed for her whole life. Especially after everything happened with Don, she carried a lot of guilt. Good times with her grandsons was a way she could make up for all the pain.

They were just everything to her. My older son, Jaycob, was born with neon red hair. We joked that he was her child. He is fair-skinned and witty, but somehow quiet at the same time. He is loving with a big heart and seems like a shy kid unless you know him. He is very much like my mom. She had such a special relationship with them that my mother wanted to tell the boys about the cancer herself. I hedged a bit, knowing that my mother did not talk about things that were difficult. We never talked about anything difficult growing up. We never talked about sickness, dying, or death. I don't know now why it was important to her to discuss the diagnosis directly with the boys.

Perhaps she was making up for lost time, saying things that she had never said because they were uncomfortable. Perhaps it was her way of alleviating some pressure or guilt for not quitting smoking or for knowing that eventually this would all come tumbling down, and she would be out of time. She was out of time to spend, time to make things right, time to tend to her angels here on earth. Whatever her reason, she was adamant that the task be hers.

My mother told Jaycob about her diagnosis at a Fourth of July barbecue. He was thirteen years old. She insisted on being alone with him, and I could hear her repeating, "It's gonna be okay" to him. Jaycob was devastated. He shut down. She was trying to hug him, and he was shutting down even further. The interaction between my mother and Jaycob went on for a good fifteen or twenty minutes. She kept coming back and wanting to hold him. The situation was painful for her. My mother didn't know that Jaycob had just completed a health class that ended with the topic of lung cancer. And sadly, he knew better than to just blindly believe that it would all be okay.

"Mom," he said to me later that day, when we were alone. His voice was small; trouble wrinkled the brow over his clear blue eyes. "No one makes it through lung cancer."

I knew he was right.

Not long after that my mother made me drive through the cemetery. In our small town passing the cemetery on the way to the grocery store, the doctor, or just about any place was inevitable. But this time was different. This time she wanted to go inside. We drove around and parked, and we left the car behind as we wandered through the aisles reading headstones. She pointed out what she wanted when the time came. She wanted a stand-up granite tombstone with a story or letter on it and a picture etched into it. An angel statue in the cemetery caught her attention. She wanted to be below it and nearby a tree so that her birds could come and visit.

Her home had a small cement slab porch. She always had bird food out at her house, and the birds would lay their eggs and let their babies hatch in her hanging plants. Every year my mom cleared out the pots of old leaves and flowers to make room for nests. The birds would come and lay their eggs, wait for them to hatch, and then stay and let the young birds grow until they could fly off. This happened for as many years as I can remember. My mother loved the time of year the birds nested and couldn't wait till they had babies.

A loveseat-sized bench sat on the front porch. We often sat out there together with my sons, her pride and joy, and watched the baby birds. Her neighborhood was peaceful, and when we sat quietly we could hear the chirping babies and even spy the momma bird watching closely, intent on protecting her little ones. All those innocent creatures brought my mother great joy, even the baby skunks we found in the drain pipe in front of her house. She fed them when she didn't see a momma.

And, here we were, under the angel statue, surveying the land where she would be laid to rest. Death was like sex, in that the topic wasn't talked about in our home. Finally, we were talking about these painful, hard, important things. Everything was changing. I remember sensing it that night. I think she did too. Time was moving differently now. We had to talk about the hard things before it was too late.

CHAPTER 3

An Officer and a Predator

I was born in Misawa, Japan in May of 1973. My biological father was in the Army, which meant we moved more frequently than the average family. This is typical with Army families, but we were anything but typical. Don was an educated man, a college graduate, and an officer. He had been a Marine before going into the Army. He wasn't anybody's dummy, as they say. He was manipulative. He would plot and plan. Everything that he did was calculated. He could turn any situation to benefit his motive for control and dominance.

For instance, when given three locations for retirement station, he chose the option farthest from extended family. Even though all our family was on the east coast, he moved us to Washington state. Far, far away from anyone who knew us, right where he wanted us.

Don was from Upstate New York. He was born and raised in Watertown, where my great-grandmother was born. Watertown is just south of the Canadian border, a small upstate town with a high unemployment rate; the entire economy centered around Fort Drum. My parents met at Fort Drum. Don proposed, and a while after agreeing, my mom had second thoughts and considered backing out of the wedding. She traveled to see my grandparents in Oklahoma. Her mother told her that if she wanted to call off the wedding, she would have to do it in person, not over the telephone. Debby traveled back to New York, intending to break it off, but never did.

We moved to Texas when I was six months old. At age four we moved to Fort Meade, Maryland. Two years later, while we were living in Maryland, Don was deployed for a year to Korea. The year Don was in Korea was blissful. My mother, brother Cory, and I had an entire year without him, which felt like heaven. We stayed up late, traveled to see family in North Carolina, laughed a lot, and slept soundly. That year was the last time I slept soundly.

When Don returned, I remember thinking that someone must have switched places with him; that my real father was in Korea and the wrong one came back. I was young enough when he left that I couldn't accurately remember what he looked like before he went to Korea or how he acted, but he was mean when he came back, venomous in his tone and explosive in his anger, especially to my brother. He would punch Cory hard in the arm in the same place, over and over, pull off his belt for any misstep, and back him up crying into his room. The beatings that my brother endured were beyond imaginable. Don seemed to have a hatred toward my brother. Don was weirdly nice to me most of the time and behaved as though I was an adult, not a child.

All the nights that followed Don's return from Korea were restless. I became a trembling, broken child, sleepless and with the perpetual worry that my father would push open the door and slink soundlessly into my room in the middle of the night. At some point in my youth I heard the phrase "sleep with one eye open," and I found myself hopeful it might be a skill I could develop. The sleeplessness explains the perpetual fog I felt in my waking hours as a child, which became a coping mechanism. I was disengaged, numbly watching my life speed by as if I were a passenger on a train.

My waking hours echoed my nights. Don would sit in his recliner, put me on his lap, spread my grandmother's brown and red afghan over the two of us and fondle me while we watched *The Brady Bunch* and *Eight is Enough*, which were my favorite shows. I loved the perfect family scenarios and how neatly all their problems could be solved by the end. I wanted to escape and go live in those television shows.

My mother sold Avon during our time in Maryland, so she attended nighttime meetings. Almost as soon as she was gone, Don would put my brother to bed and draw a bath. He gave me a wash cloth and forced me to wash his body while he said dirty things to me. I remember everything. The growl of his voice from deep in his throat. How he would tell me what to do next. The warmth of the water as he pulled my hand down under the surface and guided it onto his body. These types of incidences continued for years. From nighttime visits, runs in the wooded area nearby, and any other way he could get me alone.

We lived in Maryland until I was in sixth grade. One of those years I received a radio with a cassette recorder as a gift. A new park had just been built across the street from our house, and I remember recording "Islands in the Stream" by Dolly Parton and Kenny Rogers from the radio. Then I spoke into the mic, cassette still recording, and said that my dad was having sex with me.

Doing this felt like a way to get the secret off my shoulders and for just a moment, I felt free. I went about playing in the park with my brother, forgetting I had etched those words on the tape.

Don and the three of us were transferred to Germany in 1984. In Germany we were more isolated than ever.

CHAPTER 4

Treatment

I tried to learn as much as I could about my mother's exact form of cancer while the doctors launched into chemotherapy. The oncologist decided to treat her cancer with chemo for nine weeks, move to radiation, and then reevaluate. Some studies have indicated that redheads have a lower pain tolerance than people with other colors of hair. My mother was four feet, eight inches tall, and I know she always felt extensive pain with needles or surgery or anything medically invasive. She suffered through every needle prick, every bruise from blood draws. Even the anxiety leading up to a procedure was enough to send her into a panic. She would have to take anti-anxiety medication to make it through MRIs, CT scans, radiation, and pretty much any medical procedure.

She wasn't thrilled about the port. If you're lucky enough to not know what a port is, in this context, let me paint you a picture. A port is a small disc made of plastic or metal about the size of a quarter that sits just under the skin. A soft, thin catheter connects the port to a large vein, and chemotherapy medications are dispensed through a special needle that fits into the port. Blood can also be drawn through it for collection. You can imagine then how my small, strong-on-the-inside-but-becoming-more-frail-on-the-outside mother reacted when they told her that she was going to need a port installed. But she was resolved to do anything to try and rid her body of the cancer that had invaded and taken over all our lives.

The port was installed and became irritated and inflamed with just a couple chemo treatments. She had a severe infection and had to be hospitalized. Doctors removed the port and installed a PICC line. A peripherally inserted central catheter, or PICC line, is another type of catheter with a different type of insertion. For my mother, who hated needles, the idea that she would have one installed permanently in her skin for the foreseeable future was troubling, to say the least.

The PICC line was necessary to administer the intense antibiotics intravenously to treat her blood infection. If she wanted to leave the hospital, she would have to carry a pump so the antibiotics could dispense directly into her blood twenty-four hours a day. A week after she entered the hospital with the infection, she was discharged with her newest accessory: the pump she'd carry for the next month. This was becoming my mother's worst nightmare.

The doctors kept saying that this occurrence is rare, but we heard that many other patients who get PICC lines have the same reaction. I never felt as if we got the full picture. My mother wasn't going to go through having a port installed again, so she had to keep the PICC line. She ended up having three different PICC lines put in over the course of her treatment. Having each PICC line put in and taken out was tremendously painful.

I don't think this is how she would choose to spend her time if we had known. If only we had known.

Doctors performed more tests about halfway through the chemotherapy schedule to see how my mom's body was responding to the treatment. Bad news came. The four-and-a-half weeks of chemo wasn't doing what they had hoped, so they adjusted her treatment and ended up doing radiation parallel to the chemo. Radiation treatment or radiotherapy uses ionized radiation to kill cells in a number of types of cancer if they are localized to one area of the body. Radiation therapy is commonly applied to the cancerous tumor because of its ability to control cell growth by damaging the DNA of cancerous tissue leading to cellular death. Radiation beams are aimed from multiple angles to intersect at the tumor, sparing normal, healthy tissues such as skin or organs through which radiation must pass to treat the tumor.

Patients must stay extremely still during treatment and are immobilized with restraints made from materials that help the physicians target treatment. I'll never forget the day she went in to have her mask made and fitted. The nurse put the mask over my mother's face and used it to bolt her head to a table so that she wouldn't move when the radiation was aimed into the area near her left lung. She was so upset that afternoon. The whole process caused her so much stress that every morning before her treatments she would have to take heavy doses of anti-anxiety medication. Chemo continued, and radiation continued, and both were awful.

The radiation burnt her throat so badly that she couldn't eat or drink and could barely take her medication. The treatment caused third degree burns that made the skin on her left chest, neck, and shoulder hurt so badly that she could barely wear clothes. She couldn't handle wearing a bra, which was a serious problem for her because she was very uncomfortable being seen without one. Regardless, soft lightweight tank tops were all that she could handle.

I remember her being very excited for the last day of radiation. They called it graduation day, but it had none of the joyful pomp and circumstance that the moniker might normally invoke. They gave her the mask and a certificate for being done. Bittersweet, if you ask me. When the results came in, they seemed mixed. Clinicians at the radiation center thought the tumor had shrunk, but weren't positive, and they concluded chemo should continue. Soon after, my mother's white blood cell count fell so dramatically that she had to stop chemo and have several blood transfusions.

Her birthday and Thanksgiving were always very close together. We had Thanksgiving and her birthday together that year to lessen the number of events. She was a trooper. Those days were tough. She didn't feel very good and was always preoccupied. We never really had *her* again; from that time on, cancer ruled our lives.

My mom had yet another PICC line replacement, accompanied by more antibiotics. She missed many appointments already due to complications of taking the treatment, blood transfusions, and radiation. In a short seven months, she had already been through so much.

Normally at Christmastime we'd venture out and go shopping together, but not that year nor ever again. She had trouble finding relief in any position, let alone walking around in public. She could not go to the stores and had a hard time even thinking about it. I took her home to her house, where she hadn't been in a while. The house smelled dusty. She had been living with my grandparents since she became ill. We scoured her place and dug out all of the presents for the kids that she had been collecting over the year. They were stashed everywhere. She was notorious for abundant gifting to my boys, and she was always thinking of them. I wonder if she felt like it was her way of providing a better, happier childhood than what my brother and I had. She held so much guilt about our childhood that sometimes I wonder if she clenched it all up in her body until it turned into cancer.

We gathered things from around her house and made a list so that I could go shopping for the rest. The pain in her legs and back was so bad that she could barely sit, walk, or be. I didn't know how to provide her with any relief. Around this time I noticed a lump forming on the side of her head. She had no hair. She hadn't had hair in months because of the chemo. This lump really stood out. I wondered if it was cancer, but I didn't say anything. The doctor didn't address it either. He said that we needed to focus on the issues at hand. I didn't speak up.

CHAPTER 5

Saving Grace

In some ways, being a military kid had a lot of advantages, especially the travel. I am thankful for all the places I got to visit when I was young. Many people aren't ever able to visit foreign countries or have the advantage of visiting at such a formative age. I got to go to England with the Girl Scouts, drive in the Italian countryside, see salt mines in Switzerland, and visit France and Luxembourg. Some of the best times of my life and some of the worst happened while we were living in Germany. What an adventure. What a paradox.

I was eleven when we lived in Karlsruhe, a quaint, German town. Karlsruhe was very different from Maryland. I especially liked the way the shops and restaurants looked from the street. We went to an American elementary school on the post. The school always seemed very big. In Karlsruhe we lived on the bottom floor of an apartment building, which was an old military barracks. Our building may have housed Nazi soldiers, but the evil and trauma I experienced while I was living there couldn't have been like anything those walls had witnessed before. That building was the site of the holocaust of my innocence and the systematic torture, abuse, and outright theft of my being.

I remember that our neighbors were huge AC/DC fans. They had an artist friend of theirs draw art from an AC/DC shirt on their living room wall. They had four children and were kind. I liked them. Don was tying himself in knots, trying to keep things normal when we first moved on the economy, which in the military world means living off the post in the local community. We were new, and lot of eyes were on us. He was always like that around moving time. The predator forced to stop and learn the lay of the land. Things were rarely normal for us. What was normal anyway?

A month went by from when we moved, and I was with him in the van. We were going through the gate at the base, and he made a comment to me about the soldier at the border. "Don't you want to have sex with that guy?" he asked, glancing over to me with those narrow, sharp eyes. "You better make sure you stay thin," he said, "don't get heavy, then you can have any guy you want."

I was thirteen.

A short time later we moved to Ludwigsburg, where we would spend the next few years. Since Don was a Warrant Officer, we were living a few miles away in Officer Quarters on Stuttgarter Strasse. The scenery and structures changed when we moved to Ludwigsburg. My mother found a German restaurant right around the corner from our apartment that sold the best goulash we had ever had, the *real* kind. We moved into a great old house that had a basement and two stories, which still loom ominously in my memory. The house was private and off of the base, which made it even more isolating for us. Most of my friends lived on the post, and we didn't know any of our neighbors.

When I think about the places we lived as a family, I think about the walls and ceilings. How we were caged, hidden, enclosed, separated from each other, and engulfed in abuse. Don had pornographic magazines that he forced me to look at and read to him. I remember him setting up a television in the attic space. VCRs had just come out around this time, and I remember him campaigning with my mom for three or four months for the nearly thousand dollars this new technology cost. He would unplug it from the living room and bring it to the attic. He took me up there, and he forced me to watch pornography with him. Then he would rape me.

Don would pick me up in our Dodge Ram van after soccer or Girl Scouts, find a remote location to park, and force me into painful sex: oral, vaginal, anal, pure torture. He would tell me that my mother wasn't fulfilling his needs. He told me it was impacting him medically, and that if someone didn't take care of him, he would have to leave my mother, and we would never see her again. I wondered if anyone else's life was like this, but no one spoke of anything similar, so I kept it secret. Just as I was told.

The experiences of my life are twofold: the events that were horrific and damaging, and the opposite where in the same venue a happy positive experience would happen. For instance, that same van that held so many horrific memories carried my girl's bible study group on a journey to a Pizza Hut a few towns away. We were very excited because this was the only Pizza Hut that we would see for several years. Six or eight of us, teenage girls, excited to be out and about, laughing and having a grand time arrived at the Pizza Hut, and the van got stuck pulling into the parking garage. I was panicked, knowing that Don would be furious if something happened to the van. We jumped out of the van and ran to the back. The van's luggage rack was wedged under the height bar of the entrance. We thought quickly and told our leader to get ready to pull forward on our say-so. We jumped up and down on the bumper and made just enough space for the van to slip out of the predicament. We cheered and laughed and talked about it the rest of the night.

Throughout this odd pizza adventure, I thought about all the disgusting things that Don had done to me in that van. I sat and wondered if any other girl there had these things happening in her home. I figured they must, but I knew sex conversations were taboo and never brought it up.

Sometimes cried myself to sleep, begging whatever god watching, to let me die. What a terrible thing for a child to be praying, but what else was there? What else did I have other than pain and sleepless nights? I knew that while Don was still in my life, this horror would ever continue. That was the one truth of which I was certain.

My father was a pedophile, and he routinely sexually abused me throughout my childhood and long into my teenage years. The dictionary definition of the word "pedophile" is "an adult who is sexually attracted to young children."

In the Medical Dictionary pedophilia is listed as a "condition." When a person digs into the word and its meaning, not just emotionally, but physically and sexually, it is intriguing. What makes people like Don tick? What makes them want and carry out attacks by the means and in the fashion that they do, is an addiction. Most of us can't understand.

"Tell me that you want me. Tell me you want to be with me," he would say, adding, "tell me you love me." I never used the word "love."

Often, I would just be silent and not speak at all. It never stopped him. Fear of the known and worry about the unknown crippled me into silence. Hell was between the walls of the dwelling where we lived. Hell was in the basement, the bedroom, the living room, the van that we drove, and the woods nearby. Hell was everywhere. I died everywhere, over and over.

Don always wanted to be in control. He didn't want anyone to stay at our house, and he didn't want my brother or me to go to anyone else's house. I was thankful for rarely being allowed to have any friends at our house. I never wanted anything to happen to them. Once, when I was thirteen, and we were at Stuttgarter Strasse, my friend Becca came to stay the night. She and I planned the sleepover a few days earlier, and I was surprised when she called me the night before.

"You're coming with your dad to pick me up tomorrow, right?" she asked, "I don't really want to be alone with him."

"Why not?" My heart stopped. I knew.

"I don't know, he makes me uncomfortable," she said, "He reminds me of a rapist, or something."

We both laughed, but in a way that meant we knew some unspeakable truth.

Don was a thin man. He sat with his skinny legs crossed like a woman, his thin hair combed over and lips tightly pursed. He wore the same clothes for days at a time. He smoked like a chimney. He didn't care who you were or where you were, if he wanted to smoke he was going to smoke.

Looking back, I would be creeped out too if I just saw him on the streets. Something about his look and the way he carried himself was unsettling. I think a lot of people would have looked at him and thought something was wrong with him. He had an evil look about him. His eyes looked dead, but could pierce right through you, like he was peering into your soul, an intimacy he didn't deserve.

"I don't want to be alone with him," Becca told me on the phone. I was amazed that she was tuned in to her instincts, but I couldn't let her know that she was right. I tried on my best nonchalance and told her not to worry because I was planning to ride with him anyway to pick her up.

My mother and brother were at some sporting event that morning when Becca slept over, leaving us alone with Don. In Germany, we had the kind of doors that had old antique locks. The kind with the big skeleton key hole. Becca went into the bathroom to shower. I was walking down the hallway to the kitchen when I saw him, crouched over, watching her through the key hole in the bathroom door. I went nuts, in a moment of courage that I still can't imagine I dredged up, I dragged him into another room and told him he better never do anything like that again.

He was quiet for a moment, calculating, and then he said, "I'm an adult, and I'll do whatever I goddamn please." I was in shock, disgust spreading on my face. "If you say anything, you won't see your mother again, so you best keep your mouth shut."

I just stared at him, loathing. Why was I surprised? He was doing this to me, his own daughter, his own flesh and blood, why not someone else? And, at this point I still had no idea what he was doing to my mother and Cory.

Don was a master manipulator, so good at isolation that those walls knew many things that I didn't. Those walls witnessed too much. Amazing what they saw or heard: beatings, sexual abuse, emotional abuse, and just plain meanness, that is, horrendous, manipulative, painful, thieving meanness. The acts that went on inside of those walls literally stole childhood away. And a great deal of adulthood too.

The abuse became more frequent the longer we stayed in Germany. Don had ample access to places where he could hide us. We lived off base. He claimed no housing was available on base, and whether that was true or not I don't know. We were far from anybody who would recognize us, and traveling to places took much longer.

I was becoming more active as I got older. These activities, such as soccer, softball, Girl Scouts, were a double-edged sword. I would get to spend time out of the house with a peer group where I knew I could relax for just a few hours, but the tradeoff was that Don had more opportunities to drive me places in that van, that rolling rape box he would pull over in remote locations all over southwestern Germany.

Every time we drove some place, I knew I would be subjected to abuse. Every time. I lived in a constant state of anxiety. I was always on edge. Abuse would occur in either direction, to or from said event. I never knew which. When the abuse occurred depended on how strategic he got in convincing my mom that we needed to leave early or whatever other details he needed to fit the situation. He wasn't always the one who took me places, but I was willing to deal with it when he did because it gave me an opportunity to be gone and not be at his mercy for at least an hour or two a day, that is, besides the time I was at school.

He was aggressively abusive, but he didn't want any of us to know. He didn't want me to know he was abusing my mom. He didn't want my mom to know he was abusing my brother and me. And, I thought I was saving both my mom and brother with my own body as a sacrifice. All of it was calculated manipulation. Don's power was in keeping us separated.

Yet still, this constant hope that something would be different continued, as weird as that sounds. At times being around him was enjoyable. Moments occurred when we felt like we were a typical family. He joked around, and we felt normal. I always had this wish in the back of my mind that things would go back to what I remember as being normal. I hardly knew what normal meant. I think back to his time in Korea as a reference point for normal, but maybe that's because I was too young to remember him before that.

He would participate in something I'd feel good about, and he'd seem like a normal dad, but then on the way home he'd molest me. The tension between those two worlds was constant. I think he acted normal to draw me in. Sometimes weeks would pass between rape sessions. He would fluctuate. If I was questioning more or starting to pull away, he would leave me alone. I'd get busy and be active with more friends, and he acted normal for a while. This could go on for weeks. I can remember one span of six weeks as feeling like the longest example of this.

But overall, instances of abuse became more frequent as I got older. He was in control, and he wanted to make sure I knew it, so he threatened me in a quiet manner. "This is the way all families are," he would say. "You want me and your mom to be happy, don't you? You need to do these things so I'm happy and your mom isn't out on the street." He said things in such a way to make me think his abuse was common behavior. He played mind games that made me constantly second-guess myself.

One time I heard something inside tell me, out of nowhere and plain as day: "You're going to make it through and you're going to do great things." At the time I didn't believe it because I just kept thinking I'd never get away from him. I believed that he would continue to threaten and scare me forever.

At lunch in middle school when we would walk across the street to the Burger King Food Truck and get a sandwich, I could see his car parked amongst the trees at a distance. When I went to a football game, he was there. During softball practice, he would sit and wait. Anything that I wanted to do, whether attend youth group, spend time with friends, or go to school, he found a way to be present and to make sure that I knew he was there.

No matter where I went, he was somewhere in the distance, constantly watching, observing, and stalking. Was this the way all families were, and I just didn't know about it? All the examples I had seen on television looked and felt very different from the hell I knew in my own life. Don would constantly tell me how our life was normal. He said that the way we lived was just how families functioned, just how it was in everyone's lives. If this goes on for a while, like-- say, your whole life--you become programmed to think this must be true. This behavior was true for everyone, but people don't talk about it. My family was always very insular, very whatever-happened-at-home-stayed-at-home. That rule applied to everything from lice to chickenpox to a fight to abuse.

I went to a girls' youth group bible study while we lived in Germany. I had been practicing the words over and over, turning them over in my head multiple times, because I knew at some point the right moment to ask the question would present itself. I can't remember the topic now, after all these years, but it must have been related somehow. I think it was about parental love or fathers or something. But when this topic, whatever it was, coincided with a moment where I was starting to question things again, I spoke up.

"My father loves me different than most," I said.

The youth group leader looked at me for a moment. She was a young, red head American missionary.

"Oh Pennie, it's ok," she said, "Most dads have a special kind of love for their daughters, especially their first born."

What did that mean? I wondered. To hear her say that was reaffirming Don's actions as normal, even though it was nothing remotely normal. I examined the words in my head, "most dads have a have a special kind of love for their daughters." How was that even possible? Not only did this not make sense, but I felt shut down with the idea that no one was on my side. I wondered if Don was right.

And all at once, many different scenarios went running through my head at the same time. I envisioned all the girls on the planet going through the same thing as me. All these girls are being raped and abused by their blood fathers. That seemed impossible. This isn't sane. This is sick. I couldn't get my head around the idea. I didn't know what to do.

Don got this idea for a week-long father-daughter ski trip. "It would be fun!" he reassured. Don was in prime salesman mode. Others from his Army group were going, he insisted, but who knows if that was true at all. I would learn to ski and get to hang out with other kids my age, he told my mom. "It would be a great time for us to bond," he added adamantly.

The word "bond" stuck in my head like a thorn. All I could think about was that being alone with him for a week was going to be a living hell. He would have me cornered, able to do whatever he wanted. There was no way I was going. I had fallen for a similar ploy once before, about a year earlier when I was twelve.

We had just moved to Karlsruhe, and I was the chosen one to go to the barracks, help him pack his belongings, and clean where he had been staying before the rest of us came to Germany. I could be a "big girl" he told me, and he took me to the private quarters. I was excited. I don't know why, but I thought it would be fun. The day was spent packing books. I remember thinking that he had a lot of books. We folded and packed clothes, linens, and toiletries; cleaned the bathroom; and scrubbed the floors. I helped him load the car. The furniture stayed.

I was enjoying the normalcy when things changed quickly. The room was clean, but he left some random things out on the table, including a container of chocolate syrup. He hadn't stripped the bed yet. I didn't think about it. I wasn't paying attention because things had been okay that day.

"You need to take all your clothes off," he said to me, and he tried to force me, his twelve-year-old daughter, to kiss him. I would never, ever allow him to kiss me, and he tried that more than once. I found it to be somehow too personal. Maybe that sounds strange, considering all the ways he violated me, but that's how my brain worked. I was never okay about what he was doing to my body, but I fought harder about some things than others, and my father kissing me on the mouth like a lover was a red line I would not allow crossed.

Kissing was too intimate, even I knew that. And, although this limit might not make logical sense because he did penetrate me, this one act I felt like I could control. I would not be complicit, no matter how much he wanted to suck me in and convince me that it was okay and that this behavior and activity should be enjoyable.

That's what the bottle of chocolate syrup on the counter of that otherwise empty barracks was for. That was for me. To try and make me want him. Don wanted me to participate in this sex play like an eager lover, and he tried to excite me with sugary things I liked to eat or drink, such as pop and snacks. This man, my biological father, was trying to seduce me, playing games and convincing me to do things that would scar my deepest intimacies and impact my life for years to come.

I learned my lesson after that overnight to never again go away alone with him if I can help it. No way was I was going to spend an entire week with him alone, anywhere, anytime, anyplace.

But then something even darker occurred to me: What if he never brought me back? What if he stole me away forever? I feared being separated from my mother and brother, kept forever as a slave to "fulfill his needs," as he would say.

Don hadn't brought up the ski trip for a few weeks, but I knew that he would be pushing the topic again soon.

The timing couldn't have been better, I attended a Girl Scout meeting that effectively saved me. I love the Girl Scouts. I learned our troop would have an opportunity to join other troops and take a bus tour to England. This trip was slated for spring break, the exact time that this awful, private ski trip was planned. Could it be true? Was I out of danger? Could God have provided an opportunity to deliver me from this monster? My mind raced with possibility.

The meeting ended, and I was excited. I got even luckier because my mom came to pick me up that night. I talked her ear off the whole ride home. I told her all about the trip, airing my exuberance about how wonderful it would it be to see London with my

Girl Scout friends. "How many people get this chance?" I asked her. "Once in a lifetime," I said.

Can you imagine the look on Don's face when he heard about the trip? He was not pleased. He wasn't going along with this trip and spewed every reason he could conjure up as to why I shouldn't go. But this time my mom was steadfast, and thank goodness. I was going to England with my friends she said. "It's a once-in-a-lifetime opportunity," she said to him with a strength and determination that I had never seen in her before.

He was really pushy about it. He manipulated his words and tone to bully and said things in a way that my mom would not think anything strange about, but I would know his intention. Not only did he want me all to himself for a week, trapped on the side of some snowy mountain, but he also didn't want me around anybody else. I'm sure he was afraid that I would say something, that I would slip or confess or confide, and the abuse happening at home was going to come out.

He said that the ski trip was also a once-in-a-lifetime thing, and the trip would be with all his coworkers. "You don't ski, Debby!" he said, adding, "I've always wanted to go skiing." Then he launched into a soliloquy about how we wouldn't be in Germany for much longer and this might be our only opportunity. He became visibly upset that his plan was not working.

He became angry, but not in a fashion that clued my mom in to the situation or his intentions. He played the hurt card. She knew he was upset about it, but not for the nefarious, disgusting reasons that were the real facts. But my mom was simply adamant that I was going with the Girl Scouts because doing things with people my own age, my peers, would be good for me.

"She can go skiing anytime. End of story," my mom said, and she made it happen for me.

I was saved that night from a week of hell, although my mother had no idea at the time from what exactly she was saving me. She unknowingly protected me from this grotesque abuse that had been going on under her nose for so long. That time she saved me from the monster.

• • •

I would cry myself to sleep begging God to bring back my real father. Take this devil away, I would beg all night. Imagine the post-traumatic stress disorder I suffered. If I closed my eyes, he would come in, and if I stayed awake, he would leave me alone. But God, why allow this to happen? I couldn't figure it out. My situation was beyond reason. I begged God for relief. I was a child, and I didn't understand why God didn't listen to me and do something to stop my hell on earth. Even now I question; why a child should have to suffer the things I suffered.

I talk to survivors now: children, adults, and parents of children who have suffered the same pain, and I still can't help but wonder why our prayers aren't answered. Why are some children fated to suffer such terrible abuse? The pain that these children carry for the rest of their lives is not understandable. How does this horror take place in the presence of a benevolent and loving God? I have always felt like I had a lot of faith, but I can't let go of this one thing.

Honestly, this question shakes me, so I steer away and separate myself from religion, and I wonder and question. I know that I wouldn't be who I am today if I hadn't experienced what I did, but I will always question why God didn't stop my father from raping me. And that moment in that girls' bible study when I mentioned that my father had a different kind of love for me and nothing happened, nothing changed, and no one cared; all that occurred in God's house.

I was heartbroken. Somehow, I nurtured a flame, and over time that flame grew and revived me. The flame says love is louder. Love has to be stronger than abuse.

CHAPTER 6

Going Home

When the pain began in my mother's lower back and legs, we all assumed it was sciatica. She had been treated for it a few years earlier, and that type of thing reacts to stress and posture, so we assumed she had aggravated an old issue. Her medical team treated her for sciatica, but the pain wouldn't subside. Instead the pain worsened as the days went on.

I made it a point to talk to my mom more about the past. I don't remember now how the ski trip came up, but we talked about it and the way she had resisted his efforts. I remembered the scene as one of those moments when she really fought for me, and she didn't know what the consequences would be. That was a big deal for her during those years.

"I knew I'd end up paying for it," she told me. She rarely tried to put her foot down, and he was already plenty mean to her behind closed doors. My mother often went through cycles where she would disappear into her bedroom for days at a time. That's what the week was like before I left to go to England, and surely that continued while I was away, escaping hell incarnate at the hands of Don in the Alps or Pyrenees.

I remember having this conversation at her house before she was so sick that she had to go back into the hospital. I reached for her hand and held it. I'll never forget her crystal blue eyes, rimmed pink with sorrow for all that had happened. I thanked her and told her I loved her.

In early February, three months after the pain in her back and legs began, it became so severe that we had to take her to the emergency room. They checked her blood count. Her white count was extremely low, so she received a blood transfusion, and the admission process started. Staff set about seeing what they could administer to control the pain and try to make her comfortable. Their efforts were excruciating to watch. At some point during the intake process, they wanted to do a CAT scan and an MRI on her back and legs to find out where the pain was coming from.

My mother found it impossible to lay down flat and remain still. The pain was too severe, so after many failed attempts, they drugged her to get the scan. The back pain wasn't sciatica. The cancer had spread to her spine and was pressing on the nerves. I'll never forget sitting in the quiet of my mom's hospital room, looking across at her and through her pale skin, baldhead, and frailness, to see a strong fighter. I thought about our conversation earlier that day after we got the news that the cancer had spread and the pain in her hip was a tumor in the muscle. Cancerous cells were also found in the lymph nodes.

"Is this cancer going to kill me?" she asked me once we were alone again. Never did I imagine I would have this conversation with my mother, the strongest woman I had ever known. She told me that her biggest dream is to take her grandchildren to the beach, smoke-free, in the coming summer.

The only thing that we could get her to eat was Pizza Hut breadsticks. She asked for them daily. After several weeks, the people preparing them at Pizza Hut even knew Debby's name and would ask how she was doing.

We used to make cards with the boys for Valentine's Day, but not that year. Almost immediately after being admitted to the hospital, she began aggressive radiation treatment, except the hospital didn't have a radiation center. Instead, every day, my mother was drugged, loaded into an ambulance, and transported to the radiation clinic less than a block away. Only to be brought back again to continue battling like a warrior.

After six straight days of radiation, we measured milestones of progress in how far she could walk down a hospital hallway. Twenty feet, then rest. The doctors tell us new things we need to consider: low potassium, low magnesium. Her PICC line is infected again and possibly has to be replaced, but she's still smiling. Aunt B comes to visit from Texas. We talk about how thankful we are, and literally count our blessings with each visitor who appears. We ask friends who come calling to sign the "cheer wall," which makes her smile when she sees it, despite the excruciating pain. We anxiously await biopsy results.

"I have a lot of hopes," Mom said when she was in need of extra good thoughts and prayers, and then she'd go about listing her hopes and prayers for the future. Mom and I agreed, having hope is a good thing. She continued to fight.

On February 24th we got biopsy results, and the news was not good. After discussion with the oncologist, my mother insisted on continuing daily radiation to try and knock the cancer out. Along with radiation, aggressive chemotherapy was also part of the plan. Her decision meant another fifteen days of being loaded into an ambulance and transported in immense pain. But after test results, nothing seemed to respond to the radiation. Instead, the lump on her head grew and a new lump developed on her chest.

I journeyed down those hospital halls many times in the three weeks since my mother had been admitted. I passed many people walking, heads down, but I always said hello or in some way acknowledged them. One day while debating if I should continue this practice, I said hello to a lady walking with her head down, and I kept on going. She stopped and said, "hey," so I turned around. She thanked me for my hello and my smile. She said it was the first time she had wanted to smile in a long while. She hugged me, and we went both about our own business.

I have learned many things in this adventure called life, but what has stuck with me and been reconfirmed is that many people are going through battles of some sort; their own trials, their own personal hell. Knowing this reminds me to step outside of myself and share gladness when I can.

The next few days were rough, and we tried to take solace and joy in small things, like watching Ellen DeGeneres host the Oscars. My mom always loved to watch the Academy Awards. She loved the little gems of hope that seemed to glitter all around us. We treasured their promise. A smile, a bit of good news, a pleasant meal, a text, a card, the sunshine, that glimmer in her eye, and the hope to continue the fight. We were thankful for those things. Those tiny pearls that string together, thousands of them, can make up an entire day.

In the hospital I was reminded moment after moment to look beyond ourselves and our circumstances; to stop, notice, and smell the flowers, feel the ground beneath my feet, watch puddles gather rain, and witness smiles. Cancer is unforgiving and merciless. It's imperative to listen, look, and enjoy all those little pearls before they begin to fall away.

· · ·

One morning I arrived shortly before seven to be with my mother. She asked me to sit with her in the room and watch the clock, so I did. I waited for something grand to happen. We sat there quietly together, watching the clock. Then she broke the silence. "There," she said, "now wasn't that the slowest three minutes you have ever seen?"

I considered this for a moment and realized that those three minutes had actually felt like ten or twenty. Then I realized that this was my mom's reality: watching that big, slow clock right in front of her hospital bed tick away, day in and day out.

This was how she spent time. Sixty minutes ticked away, one by one, slipping into hours. One day blurred into the next, struggling through horrific pain and waiting for scan results, for visitors, for food, and for her next dose of pain medicine. I promised myself that I would try and fill every moment I could with her by laughing, remembering, discussing future hopes and dreams, and talking about the hard stuff.

The calendar turned from February to March, and March tore into us like a lion with the news: the cancer had spread. We sat together in the family room and talked about what we learned. The tumors had progressed down her spine and into her pelvis. Cancer was on both sides and in her sacral joints as well. The thought of the fight getting more difficult rose up around us like a canyon. We were hemmed in. Trapped.

I think my grandmother, watching her daughter go through a horrifying battle, had the hardest time. In the midst of tears, the rhetorical questions to God, the pain and fear, we all noticed a woman, alone on the other end of the couch from us in the family room. Her eyes were as red as my grandmother's. The woman cupped her face in her hands, trying to hold it together and become the smallest, most invisible thing in the room. My grandmother, in her own despair, pulled herself together and walked over to the woman, this stranger, and wrapped her arms around her. Her embrace said ever so gently that we are in this together. "I love you," she told the woman, "and I am here for you."

The woman began to cry as my grandmother held her. She just let the tears flow. At a moment when the news we had just heard regarding my mothers' battle with cancer was the most difficult yet, my grandmother told me, "We are blessed, and we must share ourselves."

Those two mothers shared many tears, some smiles, and an understanding. They were standing in stoic solidarity, supporting one another, feeling the pain of their sixty-plus-year-old daughters locked in the battle of their lives.

Around this time the oncologist pulled me aside and said that this was a very advanced case. She had only weeks left, but he didn't want to tell her.

"She still has hope," he said.

I was furious. "She is suffering," I said "The ambulance rides! The treatment! The pain!" I was shocked.

She had been in the hospital for about a month and was deteriorating quickly. She was eating less and growing lethargic and less responsive. I called Aunt B in Texas, and she came up right away. Time seemed to fly faster than ever. My older son's birthday approached, and I tried to see this all through the eyes of a child, although he was turning fourteen and wasn't little anymore.

I thought back on the last fourteen years. My mother was there for the birth of my son and cared for him since he was six weeks old. Bottles, potty training, school plays and concerts, weekly slumber parties that would go on for days, she had been there. Sports games, rock band concerts, week long vacations with just Ama and the boys that would get extended at the last minute before coming home. Through my kids' eyes, and many others, she was the grandma who could do no wrong. She was always involved. She was there.

My oldest realized the difference. He noticed specifically her pain, her eyes, her touch, and he sat and held her and talked to her, even though she called him another name and wasn't sure where she was. He set up funny movies, and they laughed together in the hospital room. He grabbed her hand and said, "Wasn't that funny?" as he chuckled, repeating the scene word for word. With his unique tenderness, love, passion, he was fully present and active in those moments because he wanted it to be time for her to remember.

The struggle of watching a loved one suffer through pain and agony is hard on everyone, but as I reflected on the toughest days, each worse than the last, I realized that everything I was feeling, seeing my mother in such severe pain, was ten times worse, maybe a thousand times worse, through the eyes of a child. At times I believed that I have had the hardest conversations, been through the hardest times and seen the worst I could possibly see, and then the next day comes.

This was one of the hardest journeys of my life. In forty years I had survived a lot and at the time I had no idea how. I don't know how to explain the peace that comforted my heart and kept my mind calm. I don't know if it's because I had already seen hell before, or because there were moments the pain meds were working and my mother was free of suffering, or because my family was together, but somehow I started to become aware of a great truth. This process was teaching me that negative thoughts and energy can suck the life out of you just as much as taking on someone else's pain and suffering.

Witnessing my mom's mental state begin to deteriorate was difficult. One day she was full of jokes, or would react oddly, for example, saying something in response to an event that had occurred minutes earlier like, "Quit talking with your mouth full. That's rude." Someone had been in her room doing just that, but minutes earlier. Once while I was trying to keep her awake to finish eating, she said in a loud voice: "Quit yelling at me, or I am not going on vacation with you."

Her journey began in late June with the cancer diagnosis; she had battled through radiation, chemo, and rapid growth of lung cancer, which was spreading through her body. I was at the edge of her bed for hours thinking about all that she had gone through. All that she was fighting for. Her journey began in late June with the cancer diagnosis; she battled through radiation and chemotherapy, neither of which could stop the rapid growth. I wondered and contemplated. I dug deep, thinking about all the prayers that had been prayed, all the verses written in cards.

I wondered at what point prayers changed. At what point do they evolve and mature? I believe this is a very personal moment that individuals have to feel for themselves. Sitting at the edge of the bed, my arms propped, and staring contentedly into her face, I felt my prayers for her change.

If you haven't been around someone at that stage of sickness, you can't be prepared for the degree to which the body is ravaged. I think this might be why some people don't go to funerals; they want to remember that person as they were.

My mom was vivacious. Always happy and loving and smiling. Even in her most depressed moments, an outsider would never have known. But she was not there anymore. My cousins came to visit with her, and I had to warn them because I knew they had never been around someone as sick. I said: you're going to see a person who looks like her somewhat, but she won't be able to have a conversation, to joke, to laugh. You won't recognize her as the same woman you've known all those years with her long red hair and makeup.

She's not the same person. I warned them that they were meeting someone bald, who may not know who is in the room, and who may not respond or could become agitated and angry at any given moment. I warned them that she basically has no control over the ability to speak or eat. The list felt endless.

Every day she was in unbearable pain and I just couldn't see her suffer anymore. At some point I had become aware that the core of her treatment was chemo and radiation, and in the oddest of medical hypocrisy, she was doomed to suffer the poisoning of her body meant to kill cancer cells. That first radiation treatment burned her neck and throat so badly, and every treatment re-injured those same wounds.

It was around the holidays when I first started to wonder if treatment was worth it. We had slogged through her birthday and Thanksgiving with pain and suffering, my mother not being able to eat or enjoy anything. Was this how she wanted the boys to remember her last Christmas? She upped the ante and opted to get more radiation treatment while in the hospital. Every day she endured getting on the gurney, being transported, getting off the gurney, receiving treatment, then going back to the hospital.

Every day she endured getting on the gurney, being transported, getting off the gurney, receiving treatment, then going back to the hospital. The pain was unbearable on account of the cancer riddled through her spine and her sacral joints. You could hear her screaming in the hallway when it was time to be moved on or off of the gurney. This is what she thought she had to do for freedom. I couldn't watch her do it anymore. But she still wasn't there yet. She still insisted on continuing the fight and poisoning herself with treatment.

Where's the line between praying for her strength and praying for an end of suffering?

I remember the very moment it all shifted for me. I was sitting at the side of her bed, my head propped on my hands, leaning my elbows on the bed. A friend snapped a photo right then, and when I see it even now I am transported to that day and the thought of how I didn't want her to suffer anymore.

That photo caught the moment when I wondered how much more her body could take. That photo caught the moment I realized that treatment wasn't worth it. I knew that day, propped on the edge of her bed, that I didn't want her to suffer anymore. It was hard. I reached for my mother's hand, and when she ever so gently squeezed mine back, I knew that it was natural for my prayers to evolve as they had. To want an end for her suffering, even though it meant she would be gone, was a merciful, wholehearted, selfless kind of love.

Tomorrow would be a new day. A fresh day. A virgin day. One that wouldn't have been touched and won't ever come back.

• • •

Jaycob and my brother's birthdays are both in March, so we did what all red-blooded Americans do, and we had a pizza party. For just a few hours we all relaxed and were just present with each other.

The folks at Pizza Hut were so fantastic and taken with Debby that they catered a birthday party in the family room right there in the hospital. The room was filled up with friends and family. Pizza Hut provided pizza, breadsticks, pop, and chicken wings for all of the patients on the entire oncology floor, plus their families and staff. That was an amazing bright spot amidst of a lot of dreariness and pain.

My brother still hadn't heard the news about our mother's prognosis and timeline. I couldn't disrupt him at the party so I waited and told him a couple of days later. I knew he would be devastated, and he was. The very next day I told my boys that Ama was very sick with the cancer and she wasn't going to make it. They were fourteen and nine at the time.

We sat in that family room at the hospital and all three of us cried together. I held their hands as tears streamed down their young faces. They looked up at me, eyes full of tears, and I felt as though a sword pierced right through my heart. The tears ran down my cheeks, and I held their hands tightly. I have always protected them, always sought to keep them from pain, but this was something I had absolutely no control over. I held them and promised them love and hugs. Then my brave boys wanted to see her, so we went back into her hospital room and spent more time with her. The television was on, and everyone stared at it, but no one cared. It was just something to look at.

It was raining when the three of us left the hospital that night, but we weren't ready to go home yet. We went to the park next door.

"There's a lot in this world we don't know," I said to them as we walked in the mist out to the playground. "There are great mysteries in the way the world works. But one thing I know for sure is that the sun will rise again tomorrow, and after that the sun will set." We sat on the swings, gently swaying. "The emotions will continue, sure. It doesn't just get better overnight, but one thing is clear: this love, this connection that you have built with your Ama, no situation, no circumstance, no cancer will ever take that bond away. Love is more powerful. That's the beautiful thing about it."

We swayed on the swings, in the rain, and cried some more.

We all have wishes for our children and do the best we can. They do not issue an owner's manual when you leave the hospital with a tiny being upon becoming a parent. A baby has no control of its appendages and can't tell its parent what it wants. You drive away from hospital roundabout, wondering if the hospital realizes that they let you take this living thing home. And, you hope that you can water it, feed it, and keep it alive.

Then they grow, and you hope and wish and pray and dream that this human being will absorb all the lessons, the love, the compassion you offer like a sponge so that they can wring themselves out later over other people's lives. My mother worked hard at this. She instilled values, the ability to love, the desire to care for people, to do good deeds, to express oneself, and to be passionate about the world and people around us. She made sure we said please and thank you, wrote thank you cards, paid attention to family when they visited, and stopped to put others in front of ourselves.

My mother believed that doing good, helping others, and loving people would make a difference in the world. As I pondered all the values she taught me, I noticed she was still showing me examples of this behavior. You'd have to know my mom to know what she was saying, but even at this point she responded to every visitor with an attempt at thanking them for coming. "Thhaa.." she would begin, then the sound would trail off, hanging there for a moment. A few weeks before she was saying, "thank you so much" and "you're such a blessing." I could see her eyes wanting to greet each person by name and ask about everyone they knew.

I will work hard so that what she created in me will live on, and I can continue to raise my children in that manner. They may create a love that will last forever.

March 13, 2014, was the last day of radiation. Her platelets were down to thirty-one. The battle continued. Mom was more comfortable with some medication changes and a bit more alert when she was awake, but this improvement was doomed to be short-lived.

I sat in her hospital room and stared at her bare feet poking out from under the blankets. She hadn't walked in weeks and kept peeling off the hospital-issued socks because they got twisted. These feet led us through learning about faith, Sunday school, youth groups, vacation bible school, and church services. I thought about all the daily prayers with my mother, the nightly blessings we shared at dinner, and how we read the Bible together. Throughout my life and in this room we talked about something bigger and mightier than we are.

In our case we learned about God and Jesus and how all-good things come from the power above. My mom, my brother, and I survived some horrific times. Clichés like: "God only gives you what you can handle," "There is a reason for everything, whether we know why or not," and "Only the strong get the tough stuff and it makes them stronger" stung. I clung onto them bitterly, thinking, "Yeah, we are the strongest, that's why we were raped as children and my mom was emotionally abused. We can handle the tough stuff."

How can an almighty God allow children to be hurt so severely, and a mother to have her worst nightmares come true? I've gone through cyclical seasons of faith throughout my life. I would lose faith and grieve, then heal and forgive, then believe again. My mother worked through her concerns, and we all came back and lived the faithful life. We struggled time and again, wondering why things had to be so hard and why all of this stuff happened. My mom would say that a reason must exist, but we don't know what it is yet.

My mother was the child, the teen, the adult who always chose the right road. She would stop and think: if her choice was wrong or was going to hurt someone, she would change it and pick the right\ road. This woman has suffered a broken heart multiple times and many of those times because she couldn't protect her children. Here we are, decades later, and she is suffering yet again. And, I hear all those trite statements: "God only gives you what you can handle," "There is a reason for everything, whether we know why or not," and "Only the strong get the tough stuff and it makes them stronger."

I sat gazing at my mother, the one that led us through life and I questioned my faith. If this all-knowing God is a being so powerful and wonderful, why would children be allowed to suffer years of pain at the hands of a parent? Why would a mother have to experience the heartbreak of her children being hurt? And, why would this angel, this wonderful person, have to suffer through such an unforgiving disease? My faith flagged a bit, and I stared at my mother and imagined her putting her hand on my shoulder and saying to me, "God doesn't give us more than we can handle."

God must think I am Goliath. Well, God, I am maxed.

March 14, 2014. We had been in the hospital for thirty-three days and my eyeballs ached. Tears came with a vengeance and now my eyes felt scratchy and dry like sandpaper. The rushing waves of tears weren't about my mother's cancer or the instability in her pain management or about the fact that her body might not be able to take any more treatment. My tears flowed, watching my family's anguish, heartbreak and love. All the people who I call family, whether by blood or choice, and loved my mother were by her bedside loving her. The waves of tears were for them.

I watched my grandfather's eyes as he observed his sickly, frail firstborn suffering in a hospital bed. I saw passion and love like none other. The type of love that a dad should have for his children. That's what real love in a father-daughter relationship looks like; a wholesome love that will never go away. My Aunt Barbara held my mother's hand with an oh-so-gentle touch, assuring my mother she would be right there and never leave her side. My cousins prayed over her and kissed her forehead, asking God for peace in her life. They headed back to Texas saying goodbye for now, and hoping it wouldn't be the last time they see her. My brother wasn't quite sure what to do. He sat near her bedside.

I sat there physically and emotionally drained, thinking of the support, love, and compassion. I knew our hearts were breaking, but I also knew that together we would make it through anything thrown our way. The next day I was a disaster. My mind fixated on how to do this all the right way. I always believed that I needed to take care of everyone else, sacrificing myself in any way to keep the peace.

No one teaches you how to navigate with grace the loss of the only parent who ever loved you. No one teaches you how to raise kids, or when to tell them that the death of someone they adore is imminent. No one gives you a manual with all the answers to all the questions, telling you when it is just the right time to share extremely difficult news with your family.

No one tells you that maybe your mother shouldn't waste the last of months of her life poisoning herself with chemotherapy or painfully burning herself with radiation from the inside out because cancer is going to kill her soon anyway.

No manual tells you the right path, what decisions you should make, how to care for everyone just the right way, how to express yourself, or how to make your thoughts understood and received. No manuals exist; what a person gets is a pat on the back that says, "Suck it up, buttercup. This is life and that's the way it goes."

No control, no changes, no Mulligans. Cancer is unforgiving, nonselective, and completely unfair. And I couldn't do anything about it.

I remember the day when the palliative care doctor came in, and finally, someone was honest with my mother about her prognosis. Palliative care doctors provide comfort from symptoms of serious illnesses parallel to treatment. We had been in the hospital for weeks and weeks, and nothing had gone well. No end was in sight.

My mother always said that she wanted to be resuscitated.

The palliative care doctor wanted to discuss the implications of that choice with us. My mother was a small woman, 4'7" with a petite frame. The impact of being resuscitated would do significant damage to her ribs and other parts of her body. The palliative care team wanted me to go first, to try and reason with her. I talked to her, but she just didn't seem to hear me. I asked the team to try.

The palliative care people told her that she had only a few weeks to live. They said that any directive to attempt to resuscitate her would prolong suffering that they just couldn't perpetuate as part of their Hippocratic Oath.

"I have so much to live for. I have so much to live for," she kept repeating.

The palliative team told her that she was going to have to go into hospice care until the end, either at another facility or at home because of insurance. I was wrecked. I couldn't let that happen to my mother. She was so upset. Her eyes were glassy and red, and her voice was exhausted. I know how tired I felt, so I can't imagine how she was still going. She wanted to spend her last days at her parents' house.

My grandparents came up to the hospital. My mom wanted to be the one who gave them the news about her new timeline and her wishes for this final step. Although she was in and out of coherency, saying these things herself to the people she loved was very important to her. My grandparents came up right away.

"Dad," she said, "I'm really sick, I'm not going to make it, but I want to come home and die at your house. I want to die with you there."

"Okay," he said, strong and stoically. That's the kind of man my grandfather was. He doesn't tell you that he loves you. He wasn't raised in that kind of environment. He never said 'I love you.' He reached out and grabbed my mom's hand and said, "We'll take care of whatever we need to take care of."

My grandmother cried. She and I had already had a conversation about this. We all knew that my mother wasn't going to be around much longer, so I broached the topic with her and my aunt about caring for my mother at home. To my dismay, they didn't think that they could handle it.

My grandmother was very concerned about her ability to adequately care for my mother at home. She worried she wouldn't be able to keep her clean and move her around. She said at the time that she thought it would be better for my mom to go to a hospice home, but the closest one was thirty minutes away. I knew at their ages and considering their own mobility issues, a place that far was unrealistic. My grandparents would not be able to get there quickly.

I stayed up all night, and the next day and night mulling over options in my head. I went to work and talked to my boss. I told him what was happening, and that I had to take care of her until the end, whenever that was.

"Take as long as you need," he said. And, I knew I was going to take her home. My job let me work remotely so that I could care for my mom as she lived out her final days under my grandparents' roof.

March 17 was day thirty-six since hospital admission. The pain wasn't quite under control, but Mom was holding her own. Her appetite lessened and her frail body had grown much weaker. Her confusion was becoming more apparent. The moments of consciousness, when she was awake and coherent, had become fewer and further between.

For the first time we knew what the future held. We met with hospice for paperwork and were approved to bring Mom home, where she asked to be. Home was where she had asked to be. Hospice would help with pain management, her comfort, and our ability to care for her. The boys took their anger and frustrations out that night at the park, swinging furiously on swings, crying, climbing monkey bars by headlight. They remembered, "Ama loves to do fun, crazy things. Let's keep doing them!"

Though the opportunities were dwindling, my sons and I reminded each other to cherish every moment we could capture. We continued to enjoy every instance that we could, despite the dark days, putting aside all the miniscule matters that meant nothing. Rather, we continually refocused on the moment at hand; love, care, and remembering what mattered. And so the journey continued.

March 19, 2014, was day thirty-eight. The day started early, at six forty-five in the morning. It seemed the sun rose quickly on the back of sleep that hadn't come until after the two in the morning. My mother slept until the doctor walked in and the questions began about how she felt. They listened to her chest and began poking at her feet. She looked at me with those unsettled eyes. I can only imagine the fear and confusion in her mind. I remember at one point when I was a kid Don had tried to convince her that all hospitals and everyone working in them were out to get her. Another master manipulation he crafted.

I ran my hand over her head, reassuring her that this invasion was almost over. This would be her last traumatic ambulance transport. I had checked everything out. The pills were safe, the intravenous medication was accounted for, and she was going home.

After weeks of searching, we had found someone who would come to the hospital to do her nails bedside. Her nails had been splashed in green and blue since the Seahawks had the Super Bowl months before, complete with team logo. The process took three hours amidst pain spells, difficulty breathing, and itching fits. At times she didn't know if she would get through the pain, but we both knew that it would be her last manicure. She was a trooper.

The day continued to be painful, uncomfortable, and anxious for my mother. Finally, the hospice doctor adjusted things, and she rested comfortably for a few hours.

Remember that manual I was looking for? It was hand-delivered, actually and entitled Caregivers Guide to the Dying Process by the Hospice Foundation of America. This book handily explains what a person's body goes through as it shuts down for death. It not only describes the physical phases, but what a family goes through; the journey, the pain, the heartache, and the life spirit loss. To me, it seemed like the author had interviewed and observed my mother, then written the book. Not exactly the manual I was looking for, but it was helpful.

The changes were occurring as listed, and finally, we knew what to do and what to watch for. My heart broke as I observed the changes in her already scant appetite and breathing as signs of the dwindling days.

I wish someone would have explained the cancer journey to us, given us a manual so that we could have known truly what to expect, right there in black and white, from the beginning. Instead we had a doctor who was not brave enough to deliver the truth.

I knew seeing my mother to the end would be one of the hardest things I ever had to do, but it was harder than hard. I could only watch and listen. I worked with the doctors, the palliative care team, and hospice, and I finally had everything setup. That piece was a challenge. The bureaucracy was a little harder than I thought it would be, but after breaking through and finding the right people at the hospital, it went more smoothly. Still, it took an entire day to get the right people at the hospital to help make it happen.

The supplies and bed were to be delivered in the morning, then we would return my mother to her parents' home, right where she wanted to be with her family and her puppy Bella. I would make sure she got that wish.

Finally, everything was in place and as if by some cosmic joke, the last day of my mother's hospitalization started off with an early morning call to my cell phone. She had ripped out her PICC line. They couldn't get her calm to clean her up or change her. I raced over. She was so out of her realm, confused, and distraught over being in the hospital. Going home was the only answer, and what she had been asking for constantly. All of my hesitations about bringing my mother home, and our ability to take care of her, were fully gone.

My life was feeling more and more surreal, like a movie that was on continuous loop, replaying over and over. The mind is a mysterious thing, and when it gets to going, sometimes getting it to stop is nearly impossible. My mother struggled like hell through some difficult times with her children, to face the battle of a lifetime against cancer. I replayed scene by scene in the theater of my mind, a behavior that in therapy is called perseverating.

As I thought over all that my mother had struggled through, and all she had wished for, I knew that her heart was smiling because at the end of the day, at the end of her life, all of her family, chosen included, came together for her. We partnered together to assure the best ending to a most amazing life, where my mother demonstrated how to love, how to really truly love, even while she was suffering. I know she couldn't have been prouder. All she had ever wanted was peace, love, kindness, and everyone to be together. And in Good Samaritan Hospital, her dreams finally came true. We were unified as a family and in service to each other and to her.

Everyone needs family or friends, volunteers, or someone by their side. They are in the battle of their life and they need compatriots. We forget that kindness doesn't have to mean moving a mountain because just giving away a smile to a stranger in passing can do wonders for both the people involved, and for all of us by proxy.

As we walked the hospital hall for the last time, I kept thinking of the nurses who said they were in awe of our family, all that we did, and how much we were there. From the day she was admitted, my mother was never alone. My heart breaks because everyone on the oncology floor deserves no less than the best, and some other patients had gone days between visitors.

On March 20, 2014, we stripped her hospital room of all the trinkets and pictures. We stripped away all the hope and prayers, and everyone headed out.

The hospital bed and oxygen were delivered to my grandparents' living room. I was trained on medicine and the pain pump. Then the ambulance drivers came, the same ones who had transported her for daily radiation treatments. The driver and attendant were so sweet, caring, and careful to keep her as comfortable as they could. I appreciated that. I followed them down the hall and watched as they loaded her into the ambulance. I pulled around, and they followed me to my grandparents' house. We still had the minor challenge of the ambulance getting lost, reprising the cosmic joke. A punch line reminding us all to just smile and take each moment as it comes. I knew that the darkness would be closing in soon, and we were going to meet it head-on. Nothing would be the same again.

CHAPTER 7

Crimes and Punishment

After several years in Germany, Don was getting ready to retire from the Army. Every day he would come back with the latest information on where we could go. My family wanted to be on the east coast, since that was where our relatives lived. The idea of going back to Maryland made me sick, but there were lots of other places we could go on the Atlantic seaboard. Lo and behold, Don came home one day and told us we were moving to Washington state.

I didn't even know Washington state was a place, or where on earth it was located. When I saw how far away it was from the east coast I couldn't believe it. No place in the mainland United States was farther from our family. We were expecting to move to the east coast, and now we would be thousands and thousands of miles away from anyone we knew and loved. It's easy to see in retrospect that he moved us out west on purpose. We were isolated, again. Completely on the other side of the country from our entire family. He isolated my mother from everyone, he isolated my brother from any friends, and he isolated me from having a normal high school life.

Wherever I would go, he would follow, lurking somewhere in the vicinity. He was a predator in every sense of the word, and I started to learn his pattern: where he would park and watch from. Even during lunch during middle school, I could find his car in the bowling alley parking lot across the street.

· · ·

I always bled after intercourse. And my mom and I didn't talk about sex in my house, so when my menstrual cycle started when I was ten years old, I didn't know what it was, or that it was normal and healthy. I learned about some things from my friends, and I quickly became scared to death that my father was going to impregnate me. I was always afraid after that.

Don bought a fishing boat. We would go out on the Puget Sound from sun up to sun down. People believed that we were going on fishing expeditions or participating in derbies or whatever, but for Don the boat was little more than a rape venue. He had me below deck as his sole audience with total privacy and all the time in the world. He had his way with oral, anal, and vaginal penetration. He still tried to kiss me on the mouth but still I refused.

These fishing derbies were the perfect cover for him to have me all alone, out on the water, and all to himself. I remember a photo of me holding a fishing pole with some puny fish hanging from it. It's probably the only fish we ever tried to catch.

Things started to shift quickly after Don retired. He was always hanging around the house. I played soccer and softball, got my driver's license and a job, and volunteered for everything possible to try and make myself scarce during daylight hours. I coached tee ball and was a Girl Scout leader. Don's rape sessions were becoming fewer and further between. I was getting busier, and he was running out of opportunities to have me isolated for long periods of time. He started showing up in my room in the night. I would wake up to him pressing his penis into my lips. I would flail around as if I were restless in my sleep, in hopes he would go away. Sometimes he would and sometimes he would be more daring and force other acts.

The summer after my sophomore year, my brother got caught growing pot plants on our roof. I watched my parents arguing in the back yard. Don pushed my mother to the ground. While I had heard him hit her through walls before, I had never seen him abuse her before this. Something snapped. I charged outside and got in between them and told him to never to touch her again, or I would kill him. A few weeks after that I saw a film starring Ted Danson where he portrayed a father who was molesting his daughter, and it all clicked. I remembered the bible teacher in Germany, how she told me that fathers love their daughters. I finally had ultimate confirmation of Don's betrayal.

I wrote a letter to my best friend Becca. Her family had left Germany for Illinois just before we moved to Washington. I wrote to her that my dad was raping me. I'm not sure exactly why I wrote the letter. I don't think I ever intended to send it. I folded it up and put it in the glovebox of my car. It was the safest place I could think of.

And then my car was broken into.

My mom had bought an awesome boom box with a triple cassette deck for me while we were in Germany. American Top 40 radio played on Sundays, and I had those cassette tapes queued up so that I could record as many songs as possible. Oh, these kids today with their on-demand streaming music. They'll never know the struggle. Well, that boom box was stolen, along with some other random things like a jacket and a grocery bag full of oven cleaner my mom asked me to pick up for her.

After my car was broken into, for what seemed like no reason, Don started saying things like, "this is normal" and talking to me with a weird secretive code like the struggle of someone who has read a journal and wants to talk to the writer about the content but can't. "No one needs to know our business," he barked out of nowhere one day, adding, "You don't want to lose your mom forever, do you?"

He never came out and said he found the letter, and the letter was still there despite the ransacked car. The letter didn't go missing, but I had no doubt that it was folded differently from how I had put it away. Clearly, someone had read it. Don would make comments that were directly tied to things I had written in the letter. There was no way he could have known them, unless he had read it.

He wanted me to feel like I was under constant surveillance, that nothing was really mine, and no place was sacred or safe. I'll never know if he decided to steal my belongings before or after he read my unsent confession.

I held on, and after I graduated high school in 1991, I had the unique opportunity to go back to Europe for a month with my Girl Scout troop. I was excited to go away for an extended amount of time to be away from him, but was so scared for my mother and brother while I was gone. Things started to unravel for Don while I was away. He was spending more and more money on junk from swap meets and flea markets, and he went on a road trip where he lost thousands of dollars in Las Vegas. His father, from whom he was estranged, died in Florida, and Don used it as an excuse for being two hours late to pick me up from the airport when I came back from Europe a month later.

I toyed with the idea of staying in Germany and looking for work. I really did like it there, despite all that terrible abuse. I was fresh out of high school and wasn't sure how I could really make that happen, but the idea sure sounded great. I loved Europe, the languages, people, and history.

Could I fake my death and stay there? I wondered. *Could I just disappear by changing my name, letting go, and leaving everything I knew behind?* That's not how this story ends, obviously. I boarded a plane and came home, disappointed, somehow heartbroken over this version of myself who I would never have an opportunity to know or fulfill, but I couldn't leave my mother and brother. Nothing is as important as family. I felt too much responsibility for them.

As I have grown, I have become a lot more transparent to those around me. I realized that I was never truly me to anyone, including myself. I didn't know who I was. I was always acting.

During the summer of 1993 I was a nanny and was going to school for photojournalism. I was the photo editor for my college newspaper and was enjoying my time. I wasn't home much, so I wasn't worrying about anything going on there. I felt free. I was determined to find my way. For a while I had considered enlisting in the Air Force to become a helicopter emergency medical technician. I was so excited about that prospect, but looking back I think I was more excited about the opportunity to get out and away from the house.

My family wasn't thrilled with the news, but they were supportive. The Air Force recruiter wanted me to lose thirty pounds. I began gaining weight after Don alluded to the preferences of that guard at the gate when I was twelve.

I never wanted to be thin. It scared me and made me feel vulnerable. Honestly, I think holding weight was a defense mechanism to keep myself insulated and safe. Maybe I thought Don wouldn't want to mess with me if I was fat, especially after all his talk. Maybe I subconsciously clung to a heavier weight as a survival tactic in case one day he decided to lock us up and try to starve us to death. I think being heavy helped me cope with all that trauma and fear.

Still the Air Force seemed more and more like it could be my escape, so I started going to the gym twice daily on top of my school and work schedule. It was the fall of 1993 and I was preparing to leave for the Air Force in February when morning I woke up with a pit in my stomach. I had an overwhelming feeling of devastation eating me up inside. I couldn't put my finger on it. I never missed work, but I called in sick that day and stayed in bed for several hours.

Don and my mother were separated by this time, but not for the reasons you'd imagine. Their separation was more about his laziness and lack of responsibility. When he retired from the Army he did nothing but sit around, smoke, and spend money. He wiped out our family's accounts and became lazy about everything: his appearance, the cleanliness of the house. He just hung around, stinking up the rec room with his cigarettes. My mom worked long hours every day. I was so glad that he was out of the house, and I barely had to see him.

The house seemed to have more air in it with him gone, figuratively and literally, but I had this sick feeling that something terrible was going to happen. I knew that I had to somehow get out of enlisting in the Air Force. I couldn't see how they were going to let me out, though, because I was signed up. I had done the intake, and everything was set for me to go. But I knew that my mother and brother were going to need me sometime. I didn't know the why or what for, but I knew that I had never felt anything like this before in my life. Something was going to happen.

So, I got up my gumption and went down to the recruiter's office. I explained that my mother was having a terrible time with my brother, and I was just worried sick about leaving right now. The recruiter stared at me. He wasn't responding, so I turned on the faucet and let the tears roll out. I went on and on about my family needing me, about the hardship of my mother being a single mom and all the trouble my brother was suddenly getting into. The fact was that after Cory got caught growing pot, he had continued acting out until he ended up in juvenile hall.

"You have to let me out. Please," I begged, crying and working myself up as much as I could make myself.

"Miss, you are enlisted. If I discharge you now, you will never be able to join again."

I know he meant it as a threat, but I found it comforting. I signed the papers, ran to my car, and never looked back. I knew that I couldn't run from my problems, not by changing my name and moving to Germany and not by enlisting in the military. Run and they will find you. Trust me, they always do. Just look in the mirror.

• • •

I used to spend a lot of time contemplating that if I had a sister, I would have had to protect her. But since I had a brother, I was sure he was safe. No way was he being sexually abused I thought. I spent hours contemplating the idea, convinced that a man would never do the things Don did to me to a boy. Especially not if I was sacrificing myself. In my head it was all about protecting them.

The facade began to fall apart shortly after I backed out of enlisting in the Air Force. I was at work when the phone rang. My mother was on the other end, and I could tell by her tone that something was terribly wrong. She told me that she needed me, that she didn't know what to do, and asked me to come home quickly, all in a quiet, controlled tone of voice that I recognized meant she was very upset.

My mind raced. Anxiety and panic tried to make their way into my limbs. Was it something with my brother, I wondered. Maybe my grandparents or someone else in the family was ill? I was imagining the worst of all options. No matter how terrible my thoughts were, the reality was to be much worse. I got out of work quickly. I let my boss know that there was an emergency, and I needed to get home right away. He didn't object. I walked up the circular drive to my mom's front porch. I saw her and Cory through the window, sitting at the dining room table, waiting for me to arrive. *Okay*, I think to myself, *he's not in jail, maybe it's not as bad as I thought.* I slowly opened the door and entered with caution, unsure of what I was walking into.

My mother was on one side of the dining room table, and my brother on the other. My eyes moved back and forth between the two, surveying the situation. I pulled a chair out slowly and sat down. I could tell they had both been crying, their eyes were red and raw and puffy. Still, I wasn't sure what was going on yet. I looked at my mother and opened my mouth to ask what was happening, but before I could, she fought through her tears to inform me that my brother had taken the car without permission.

He had planned on beating her home from work, but she was there just minutes before he got back. She confronted him right away. He was only fifteen and too young to drive, plus taking the car without permission was really stealing, she reminded him. If he didn't get on the straight and narrow, she was going to make him go live with our father.

Cory absolutely panicked and began to sob. Then he started talking. One after the other, words came tumbling out, each one barreling into my mother. Pummeling, piercing right through her heart. He explained that she couldn't make him live with that bastard, that he would run away before anyone made him share a roof with that man ever again. A horrific picture started to come into focus. Our father had been abusing my brother physically, verbally, emotionally, and sexually for years.

Don had always had this hate for Cory. He would beat Cory down and tell him that boys are worth nothing and that he would never become anything worthwhile. I see now in hindsight how it was true, how our father would become fixated on the strangest things. I remember one particular night he became so angry that my brother wasn't wearing an undershirt that he busted up the entire dinner table. I never realized until many years later that he was obsessed with requiring Cory to wear undershirts because Don didn't want anyone to see the marks he'd left on his son, and an undershirt would mask the injuries.

I didn't realize it at the time, but my brother wouldn't ever take his shirt off in public. If we were at a store and my mom wanted my brother to try on a shirt, he would get very upset about changing in front of people. We always thought he was just modest, but in reality, he was hiding something just as terrible as I was. I just couldn't believe that Don was sexually abusing us in the same home, and none of us knew this was happening to the other. This was the work of a top-notch psychopath.

My mother could barely get the words out as she recounted confronting Cory. She couldn't look me in the eyes. I sat there and let them both sob, taking it all in. I couldn't bear to hear the stories. I couldn't bear to feel the pain that enshrouded my family. The pain was eating them up. This was only the beginning, and I knew things were going to get worse. Then the question came, the one that I had been avoiding since age five.

"Has he done anything to you, Pennie?"

I stopped in my tracks. I couldn't think, I couldn't process, I couldn't speak. Time stood still, and I felt like no one else was in the room. Everything boiled down to me and my thoughts. I wanted to tell them and finally relieve myself of my burden, but I stopped myself. I had to protect my mother just a little longer. Even if just for tonight. I had to make sure she had just one night to process what she learned about my brother and get herself together to be strong for what was to come.

So, I lied to her and said, "No."

Time stood still, and the next two days were brutal. You might be wondering how my mother didn't know what he was doing to you. In one word: abuse. My mother was terribly abused. My father was so manipulative and calculating. He emotionally abused her to the point that she didn't know if she was coming or going. I watched him beat her down day after day, talk to her like trash. He was educated and an officer in the military. He knew exactly what he was doing. He knew all the tricks, all the words, all the right things to say. I don't know how my mother finally mustered the strength to leave him after all those years.

She was even stronger than I could have imagined when she called him that night after my brother's unloading. He was in New York dealing with his sick mother. He would be traveling back the next day, but she couldn't stop herself from calling and confronting him. He told her that my brother deserved it. That Cory had asked for it and that she would never understand. The whole next day I was in shock thinking about the revelations. All those years I had believed that my brother wasn't touched on account of his gender, but I was completely wrong, so utterly wrong. Eventually my brother would turn to drugs for comfort, and then to the streets. This young man who had so much potential had been destroyed, made virtually unable to live in society.

My mother knew I planned to pick up Don at the airport and begged me not to, but I had to confront him, face to face, about what he had done to Cory. The ride was silent. Fifteen, twenty minutes passed, and I sat seething. I don't know how I kept from ripping the steering wheel from the dashboard. I swear that old Honda Accord probably has permanent dents from my grip marks. Finally, staring straight ahead, I asked him, "How could you hurt your son?"

His answer was short, and curt, and would change my life forever. "He asked for it," he said.

That was Don's reply: "He asked for it."

I thought I would vomit right there in the car. This man, this grown man of fifty-plus years, sat there and had the nerve to tell me that my young, innocent brother "asked for it." I pulled the car over and told him to get out. I didn't think twice about leaving him in the dark on the side of that freeway. Unfortunately, we were only 200 yards from his exit. I wish I had said something sooner so that he had even farther to walk.

Today, after devoting many years of my energy into research, I understand a bit more about child molesters, pedophiles, and perpetrators of incest, but nothing can change how disgusted I was by Don. I was even more disgusted by his inclusion of my brother in this terrible game than of just my own abuse. Knowing what horrors, I had endured in my own physical body by his hands, learning of my brother's abuse pushed me over the edge.

My mother knew that I wasn't telling the truth that night when my brother confessed. She knew he had been abusing me too. She hounded me about it, and finally, after two days of her asking me if he had abused me, I confessed.

I just couldn't tell her that first night. I knew deep in my soul that she couldn't have taken anymore right at that moment. She was already devastated. This woman who tried so hard to protect us. We watched G-rated movies until we were in our teens. She tried to protect us from people she didn't know and kept tabs on where we were all the time. She tried, but as she would later say, "I worked so hard to protect you from the outside, but I couldn't protect you from the inside."

On September 9, 1993, my mother called the police, and eighteen years after Don first fondled me under that afghan, a bench warrant was issued for my father's arrest. I had endured eighteen years of torture, eighteen years of trying to protect my family with my own body. He was finally going to be held accountable for his disgusting, vile actions.

We were immediately questioned in the aftermath of the police report, and although it had been more than two years since Don last penetrated me, I was subject to physical exams to validate the abuse. Rape kits where I was swabbed and prodded and every inch of my body was photographed. I spoke words that I had never verbalized before in one-on-one interviews with investigators and detectives I had just met, and they had me hand write my answers.

Telling them everything I could about the abuse was painful. I described the physical horrors, the emotional trauma, and how he manipulated me into keeping secrets. I told them how he had told me that if I told my mother, bad things would happen. How he told me that he couldn't live without me and that I needed to help keep his marriage to my mother going. Reliving every moment, as much as I could remember from the past eighteen years. My account filled twenty pages.

And of course, Cory was doing exact the same. The rape kit devastated him.

For weeks we would receive follow-up calls from detectives, asking for more details, and then from counselors and social workers. We went through hours of interviews, pages upon pages of questions, individual counseling, and family counseling. Whether I was telling the truth and the goodness of my character were questioned over and over. I became sick of people asking me if that was what really happened or not. After four or five months of authorities collecting every last detail, everything was pulled together, and adjudication began.

• • •

Don was charged with two counts each of child rape in the first degree, two counts of child rape in the second degree, and two counts of child rape in the third degree. Basically, these were meant to cover us during all the different age ranges for the crimes perpetrated against both my brother and me with the idea that trying the cases together would produce a greater impact. Don pled down to one count of child rape in the first degree. That's intercourse with a child under the age of twelve, which is a Class A Felony in Washington state.

The prosecuting attorney was concerned about going to trial with a case like ours. Jurors, or humans in general, often cannot comprehend crimes like the ones Don perpetrated happening to children. Acts like his are so incongruent with most people's realities that they simply cannot believe it could happen. Add to that, Don was smart, educated, and manipulative. He served in a respected position as an officer in the military, and he was well-liked in the community. The prosecutor was concerned that the crime was so shocking that Don might actually be found not guilty, so they recommended that we accept the plea bargain to child rape in the first degree and leave it at that until sentencing day when my brother and I would speak, and the prosecutor could petition the judge for the most severe sentence possible.

In my mind, the hearing felt like a trial because all the attorneys spoke and we spoke, but this was a sentencing. Don had pled down to a lesser charge, and now we would see how much time he would have to serve. The courtroom was the plain, austere type you'd expect. The judge had an area with the court reporters in front, a jury box to the right, and the attorneys' tables. A waist-high wall separated a gallery of pews for spectators from the business area of the room.

I walked in and scoured the courtroom to see who was there. I saw my grandparents, my mother, my brother, and others who were there for their own situations. This was a docket courtroom, meaning more than one case was being heard that day. A long hallway ran along the waist-high wall to the left of the gallery, where we were all seated. What none of us realized was that the door at the back of the long hallway was connected to the jail. The door in the back of the room opened, and in walked an officer, followed by a second officer, and then prisoners filed in behind them. Two men in blue jumpsuits walked in, and Don followed them, wearing an orange jumpsuit and plastic sandals.

I will never forget my mother's reaction when the corrections officer brought him through the door. We weren't prepared to see Don escorted into the courtroom, hands and feet shackled, shuffling his way in the door. This was the first time she had seen him since his trip to New York when my brother confessed, and she had to call the police to tell them that her babies had been sexually, physically, and emotionally abused by their father, her husband. And, that she had no idea it was all going on in her very home. He walked past her in that orange suit with his feet and hands chained together, staring a cold devil stare.

My mother began to have trouble breathing. She made strange noises and struggled. Don was seated across from us, staring us down, looking more and more like a caged demon. The devil never blinked, his eyes fixated on us as though we were the criminals in the room. My mother began to hyperventilate, her eyes rolled into the back of her head, and she nearly passed out. We quickly rushed her out of the courtroom and into the lobby. Getting back in there right away was very important. I didn't want him to think he had any more power over us in that moment.

There were several cases on the list in front of ours, which gave my mother time to compose herself. She gathered her wits, and we reentered the courtroom together. He was seated in the jury box with the rest of the prisoners awaiting sentencing. They were away from us, but not out of view. We could see each other, and Don did not seem to take his eyes off of me the entire time. Our case was called to be heard.

The defending attorney spoke, then the prosecutor spoke. Then, as victims, my brother and I had an opportunity to address the court, so the judge could take our statements into consideration when deciding the sentence. My brother spoke, and I was so nervous that I don't remember anything he said. Then it was my turn. I walked to the judge's stand. The judge asked me to say my name and age and to spell it. I did, and my voice shook.

The prosecutor stood between the devil and me, blocking the stare that still hadn't subsided. Don wouldn't take his eyes off me the entire time, and I just stared at the judge. *You haven't destroyed me yet*, I thought to myself, *and I'm sure as hell not going to let you start now.* The prosecutor spoke directly to the judge, turning occasionally to look at Don. I don't know how the prosecutor knew just where to stand, but he intentionally stepped between us to interrupt Don's line of sight. It was perfect. The judge asked me directly if the summary of facts that the prosecutor had presented was true.

"Yes." I replied

He said that my father was pleading guilty to lesser charges and how did I feel about that. This was the first time I had spoken publicly about this. My voice shook as I gave my testimony. "Your honor," I said, "This man had no mercy on my brother or me for a combined amount of thirty-three years. He is extremely violent, and he has robbed us of our childhood. Please sir, have no mercy upon him as he has had no mercy on us. That is all, your honor."

I turned around to him still staring at me, and I stared back and went back to my seat. After our testimony, the prosecutor then came back to explain to the judge why this situation deserved an exceptional sentence. Typical sentencing is 102 to 104 months. Prosecutors recommended Don receive double, that is, 208 months or seventeen years. The judge reviewed everything and said that based on this case, the things the offender has said, what the offender's children have said, "We're foregoing the regular sentence and going with the recommended exceptional sentence of seventeen years."

Seventeen years was an exceptional sentence, and somehow, still shy of how long he had abused me.

That was a tough day. I had a tough lifetime under Don's reign of terror. His control over us had finally ended. We had hardly begun to heal, but some feeling of vindication was a start.

We went back to my mom's house, and I held her as she cried hysterically in her living room. We ate spaghetti together. Ragu. No onions.

CHAPTER 8

I'll Fly Away

My mother came home from the hospital seven days before she died.

I connected with the hospice people and arranged for all the medical equipment. The nurses at the hospital told me what we needed. I'm a do-what-you-gotta-do kind of person, so I got into that mode, made a list, and got through it. I didn't allow myself to feel any emotion about how hard it all was. I think it was maybe even a year after she passed before I had a good cry.

My grandparents' house was simple but had lots of trinkets and collectables that got cleared out, along with the furniture. The empty room showed off my grandfather's craftsmanship. Thanks to him, the walls were a fancy combination of wallpaper and peach-tone paint. We placed her bed along the windows so that if she were coherent, she could look out and see trees and the street, sidewalk, driveway, and bird feeders. Her rescue dog Baby Bella quickly took to the situation and curled up into that bed in the windowed corner of the living room.

The oxygen, the hospital bed with the do not resuscitate notice taped to the end, and the pain pump all moved into that room. The kitchen was a staging area of medicine, charts, hygiene supplies, and cleaning supplies. When I was not caring for her, I was working. The agreement with my employer was that when I could, I would get online and work. I have a crazy work ethic, which maybe is linked to my drive to keep everyone happy.

I would sit by her bed, between visitors, hit her pain button, and just kind of zone out into my work world, keeping myself from thinking about anything else. Work was a relief, really. I had projects, regular reports, and staff for whom I was still responsible. Work prevented me from having to feel my feelings. Work was a safe haven in thirty-minute increments until it was time to push my mom's pain medicine trigger again.

I was working on funeral and burial arrangements at that time too. My mom, as it turned out, didn't want to have a service in a funeral home. We would bring her back to the house for three days and make party arrangements. We watched her sleeping there in her hospital bed. The thing was the size of an aircraft carrier and we marveled at how small she was within it.

My grandmother clucked her tongue. "She'll be leaving for heaven from a place where love abounds, where she belongs, home."

We watched my mom deteriorate slowly in that hospital room, but now that she was out and among all our familiar, civilian things, she appeared even further gone. I looked around the room at her loving parents and watched them for a moment. Parents aren't supposed to outlive their children. They're just not, and doing so is against all natural order. A parent's pain is profound when a child is taken from them. No parent ever thinks this will happen. My grandparents' eyes sparkled with love and tears as they held their daughter' hand.

I know the pain of watching my mother dwindle away. I can't imagine the pain of losing a child. I pray I never will. But again, just as in childhood, my faith was tested. Heaven help me when some blind believer tells me, "There's a reason, you just don't know it yet," or "Don't worry, you are only given what you can handle." I feel sick to death of platitudes.

During my mother's first night out of the hospital in over six weeks, my heart ached not for what was ahead for my mother, but what was ahead for those of us left behind. For the parents who loved her unconditionally, the grandchildren who loved her like their own mother, her children who were forever grateful for her strength and bravery, her sister who looked up to her and cherished their friendship, and for everyone with whom my mother had ever come in contact. We were all better for having known her. She was truly one of a kind. She was a good one. I can only hope to be half as amazing as my mother.

As the weeks wound down to days, and days into hours, I reflected on the deep gratitude I had, and always would have, for forty-one years with my mother, for family who have been by our sides, for friends with hearts the size of the universe, and for the ridiculous life circumstances that have made me who I am and was. I will always be proud to be her daughter, and I will always strive to make her proud of me in return.

"The things that matter most in our lives are not fantastic or grand. They are the moments when we touch one another, when we are there in the most attentive or caring way." Jack Kornfield

Day forty-two came, and to hell with "Kumbaya" because my mother dying of cancer in front of me was all so damn unfair. Whether you believe in one God, many gods, some other higher power, or even nothing at all, dying from cancer is unfair. My son Jaycob that night said: "Ama was given a cookie, then kicked in the shins and had her cookie stolen, and it's not fair."

That's true, kid. Life ain't fair, I thought.

Years earlier my mom had to fire a girl from the store she managed at Fort Lewis because the girl had made three major mistakes on the cash register. Somehow, within six months, that girl's mother ended up becoming my mom's boss. That woman made my mom's life very uncomfortable. She took away the summer store, which meant no more Miss Debby for all those soldiers. Instead, Mom was reassigned to work nights at a small convenience store at the other end of the base as retribution.

Miss Debby took it for about six or eight months before one morning she completely snapped. I knew she was having a rough time. I knew this woman was nasty to my mom and said terribly mean and hurtful things to her. My mom had earned special awards and commendations left and right for customer service. Soldiers wrote letters about how Miss Debby had gone over and above to get them all the uniform pieces they needed to go to Saudi Arabia, or wherever they needed to go. She always exceeded expectations and shined on performance reviews. To this day I don't know what made her do it, but one day she walked in and told everyone in the store that she was retiring, effective immediately. Miss Debby dropped the mic and walked out.

Several of my mom's friends didn't even know she had cancer until right at the end when I called the base to tell one of her good friends. People said that after she retired, they had called, but my mom never answered or replied. I think not responding was her way of coping with the loss. She didn't want to know any stories or be reminded of what she no longer had, so she isolated herself.

I called her old job on base, two or three weeks before we took her home. Some of her coworkers came to the hospital, and she was still a little coherent; some came after she was already home. One coworker came and brought the terrible boss, from her work, with her. They just showed up, out of the blue. Well, my grandmother recognized her, jumped up, and charged outside. I've never seen her move so fast! She stood there on her porch, arms crossed under the cement gray northwestern sky.

"You're not welcome in my home," she told the woman. "You treated my daughter terribly," she said, pointing at the woman. "You don't get to see her like this. You don't get the opportunity to say anything to her in this state, right before she's about to pass. Go away and don't come back."

My mother was deteriorating so rapidly that even just a gap of twelve hours exposed obvious changes. Her skin was pale and fragile, her cheek bones protruded, her chest looked like a washboard. There wasn't much left of her. Family came and went. Friends visited and departed. I thought about how selfish we humans can be, myself included. Human nature makes us want people to keep fighting. We want people to be well and happy and live forever, gain, gain, gain, and no loss.

We need to step back, look at ourselves, and intentionally even if temporarily, look beyond personal selfishness and wake up to look reality in the face. Then we can decide what is best for the one lying in the bed. Selfishness in this realm is human nature. At what point should we release our wants, our pain, and our fears? At what point should we step out of selfishness and move into self*less*ness? Because doing that is going to hurt, be painful and terribly hard to watch. But as a circle of family and friends, we need to rejoice with all the memories and reflect on all the fun times through our tears.

I was sitting in the recliner next to my mother, her breathing becoming more and more labored. The hospice nurse was visiting. She said my mother's heart rate was elevating and her oxygen level in her blood was decreasing. She turned to me and said, "It won't be long now."

We had gone from years to months to weeks to days to hours very rapidly. And, how did the hospice nurse know everything, I wondered. I could not help but think to myself that this was not fair. For ten months oncologists allowed my mother to put herself through a living hell with torturous treatment options. Now this hospice nurse seemed to know everything that was happening to my mother's body like clockwork. Not so long ago my mother had much to live for, many to love, and much living yet to do.

I withstood this avalanche, this onslaught of negative thoughts, and took a breath to regroup. I thought about all my friends who have lost a mother or father when they were younger than I was right then. I counted my blessings because I had been lucky enough to have some to count. I thought to myself: *at least I had this time*. In the months since her initial diagnosis, my mother and I had been talking, in cars and hospital rooms, but I realized that these hours and minutes were waning.

She had stopped wanting anything by mouth five days before. Even though I knew what was going to happen, I had a hard time with this development. Even when she was in so much pain from the radiation, she needed to eat and drink. When my mom was coherent, she would say, "I want to go home." The first few days we had been in the house, she had been adamant about it.

My aunt was struggling. She had not let my mom know she was going to be okay without her older sister. She said that if she could crawl into the coffin with my mother, she would go with her, but my mom was still alive. Finally, she said, "Debby, it's okay, I'm going to be okay, you can go." My aunt saying that was a milestone, I felt. My mom needed to hear that each of us were going to be ok, so that she could let go.

The time had come to be sure everything that needed to be said got out, no holding back. "Be brave," I told myself, "say whatever you need to, let the words fall out honestly."

So, the next to last night of my mother's life, was dedicated to intentional, peaceful, and loving words. I made sure I knew all of her wishes that night, and I promised her that we would have a great big "blue jean dance party," just as she had requested for her memorial service. She wanted a party. She wanted people to be happy. She insisted.

That night, I watched her face while she slept. I imagined her with her curly red hair, smile of encouragement, and glimmer of love. I thought back to the times she had put on a phony voice in order to sound stern. She reminded me that despite her size that "big things come in small packages" and she could still "spank my butt." She was never convincingly mean, but she tried.

And though we went through hell on earth together, she had been very protective. When we lived on-base she wouldn't let me go off on the economy like other kids I knew my same age who were allowed to be more independent. When I complained, she told me she was responsible for me, not the other kids. Yes, momma tried.

As I looked around at all our family and friends, together, doing whatever needed to be done to support my mom as fully as possible, I felt the love. I felt the love abound, the love that she started in us and shared with us. I felt the undying love she had for her parents, sister, grandchildren, nieces, friends, and coworkers.

What an amazing mom you were to care for and love us so deeply, I thought to myself as I looked at her.

I saw her as she had always been, in her purest form: a strong, passionate woman who fought for what she knew was right; a mother who cherished her children more than anything in life; and these past months as a heart warrior, fighting this horrible disease. I saw the woman who never let a disease define her, who never let circumstance direct her course, and who never let another person make her feel inferior. She lay here, continuing to hold onto life, rapid pulse, changing breath, and a slight, lingering fever. I wanted her to know that she would win this battle because she was a brave fighter who has decided on peace.

Cancer would not win. My mother's heart had already won.

I whispered to her that I wanted her to have peace that surpassed the knowable or understandable. I told her that we would take care of each other and never let her legacy vanish. Her legacy was that her heart, the energy field of her heart, and all the ways she had touched people were bigger than the quivering physical organ sitting in her chest. This truth would be my strength, my aim, and my driving force, and from that day forward I would ask myself: "What are you filling your heart with? The pain, or the blessings underneath the pain?" Sometimes the most incredibly difficult days are the ones with the blessings buried beneath. Seeds we sow into that fertile ground of our hearts is what we shall reap and harvest.

People came to reconnect one final time or just sit around the room and share stories or talk about old times around her. I was happy people had a chance to express themselves and feel connected to her one last time while she was alive. I'm not sure how much of it she heard or understood. She wasn't lucid at all during the day before she passed. My boys had ample time and space to talk with her throughout this time. In those last days, for them, nothing remained to say except that they loved her. They told her that, held her hand, and let her know they were there.

We talked about the hard stuff. For the first time in my life I wanted to make sure of it. No more leaving things unsaid. No more unasked questions. No more quiet acquiescence. That was all over.

. . .

The day my mother earned her wings started as usual: Family and friends buzzed around, staying as near to my mother as we all possibly could. Over the past week I would wake a few times during the night to give her an extra dose of pain medicine before her body knew the medicine was missing, but the night before she passed I had stayed up all night. I wanted to be awake for her, and I held her hand in the night to make sure she was still there.

I had been running on adrenaline, trying to care for my mother at home and watching her body deteriorate for a week. Something had been different about that day; I could feel it from the moment I woke up. I knew it was her last day: the crescendo, the precipice, the threshold from one version of life to the next. We all stayed close, and if one of us left the room for any reason, we were quick to return. I was feeling anxious and called the hospice nurse to ask questions.

"Remember your road map, remember the phases," she reassured me.

We hung up, and that's when my mom's body expelled a bunch of waste. We cleaned her up, and in my heart, I knew the time was near. We wanted to pamper her as much as we could in her last moments in this physical world. My cousin painted her toenails to match her manicure. We rubbed her hands, washed down her face, and massaged lotion onto her legs and arms. Her extremities were cold despite her temperature being elevated with fever. Her heart rate was off the charts. Her breathing changed drastically and took on more of an animalistic nature. Her mouth was moving in sort of a gasp, like a fish struggling on land. Her spirit had no use for this body any longer.

We all gathered around my mother's bed. Everyone holding onto her and holding onto each other. *Jeopardy* was playing on the television in the background. We talked to her, assured her we loved her, and promised to take care of each other. I asked a friend of mine to take the boys home because I was worried. I had heard many stories about death being a violent event, where the dying person flailed around. I should have known that in the case of my mom it wouldn't be like that; she was calm. I wish they had been with us because as hard as death is to witness, the transcendence is beautiful.

Her breathing became shallower, the space between her breaths grew further and further apart. My cousin told my mother that her nails were done and everything was set up just right for whenever she was ready. I counted the seconds in between each slowing breath just like the hospice nurse had coached me to do. The space between them grew longer and longer. One single tear fell from her eye, and with a final gasp, an opening almost, a spasm, her muscles relaxed. It was 7:55 p.m. Wednesday, March 26. My mother was at peace.

"She's gone" I said, eyes wet with the intensity of the moment. One hand held hers, the other stroked her forehead. I hadn't noticed, but my uncle had jumped up and grabbed a CD he had made and brought with him from Texas. He slipped the disc into a stereo, and it began playing a sweet, sweet song that always brought out the southern side of her and that she used to hum while cooking in the kitchen.

I'll fly away, Oh Glory.
I'll fly away, in the morning.
When I die, Hallelujah, by and by, I'll fly away.

When the shadows of this life have gone, I'll fly away;
Like a bird from prison bars has flown, I'll fly away.

I'll fly away, Oh Glory.
I'll fly away, in the morning.
When I die, Hallelujah, by and by, I'll fly away.

The song played, and we all sang around her, celebrating through the tears because we knew that although we would miss her, she was free from pain. It's only a cliché until you've witnessed someone you cherish suffer like that.

As the song ended, my grandfather surprised us by insisting everyone pull out our cell phones and get all the "greats," that is, my three great aunts and great uncle from the hills of North Carolina, on speakerphone. Cell phones came to life around the room, and amidst the tears and sniffles, "I'll Fly Away" played again. Family and loved ones sang and clapped along together across miles and time zones. I felt the union of my family and the bond in our gathering and celebration of life.

That was it. It was more peaceful than I ever could have imagined such a life-changing event could be. No flailing happened, no violence. All the things I had worried about my sons seeing hadn't happened. I called home and had them come back over. I then called my brother, so that he knew right away. I could hear the devastation in his voice. I told him that he should come, so that he could see her before the funeral home came. He arrived shortly there after.

We linked together and surrounded her bed, circling all the way around it without a space between us. We wanted to be together. My family wanted to keep her there. Still not ready to let her go, my grandmother and my aunt kept bargaining, asking if we could just wait a few more minutes, so we did.

Finally, I realized that I would have to make the call to the funeral director. It would take them an hour to get there. It was 11:30 at night when I called, and nearly one in the morning when they finally took her body away.

• • •

"Don't be burying ten thousand dollars," my mother said. She was adamant about not having a fancy casket. Miss Debby worked very hard for every penny, and she didn't want fancy because fancy was frivolous. Blue and cheap were her rules. She talked about plenty of things in the lead up to her transition from this physical life. We talked about the abuse, the struggle of living in perpetual victimhood, and our hopes for the future. But one thing we never talked about was our apparent family tradition of a home funeral.

I have never attended a viewing in the home before, despite it being a family tradition. As a military kid, the chances of being at home for a funeral were slim. I wasn't aware of this "family tradition" until two days before my mom passed away. We were in the kitchen. The coffee pot was going. My aunt was standing at the stove, and my grandmother said, "Are you bringing your mother back?" She hadn't passed yet. She was still alive.

I looked at her, perplexed. She repeated herself, and then I said, "I don't know what these words mean, can you help me understand?"

My grandmother said, "Before she's buried, for the viewing. Are you bringing your mom back here before she's buried?"

I still felt clueless.

"In the Barker family," started my grandmother, "the coffin is brought back to the house for an in-the-house viewing, a wake."

In all our talking, my mom had never mentioned this one detail. Par for the course, I suppose. We didn't have relationships with any funeral homes, transplanted to Washington state such as we were. There were three funeral homes in the general area, and, on a recommendation, we selected a place one town over.

I called the funeral home, skeptical of what my family wanted, and they confirmed it was a real thing.

"It don't happen a lot around here but, we've done them," the person on the telephone said.

I asked the Funeral Director what the maximum amount of time she could be back at the house was. I knew my family and how attached we were, and I imagined that even though her body was prepped, it was flesh and bone and time would be of the essence.

"Forty-eight hours," the person said.

I got rid of all the equipment, everything hospital related, and prepared the room for her to return in a coffin. Later that day my aunt came with me to the funeral home to finalize the remaining details. It was a little brick house in a residential community. I didn't want to know what those walls had seen. Aunt B asked if she could see my mother's body. They said, no, that they were in the middle of preparing it. My aunt was upset that they wouldn't let her see her sister. My mother's body was brought back to the house the next day, and we were as ready as we'd ever be. Two last days to honor her and celebrate our goodbyes.

• • •

When you have a home wake, the funeral people show up in a black minivan, not the white one that picked her up. This way they don't freak out the neighborhood with a hearse arriving and unloading a coffin onto the front lawn. Instead, they discreetly pull up, and if possible, they drive around as far from the street as they can. We carried her the rest of the way, through the backyard and the sliding patio doors you'd never imagine would be used for such an occasion. This was also favorable because of the angles of the entryway and a general distaste for carrying a coffin into the house through the front door.

They rolled her coffin in and took some time alone in the room to set her up because of "transportation," said the driver. When she was ready, they had me go in first. The scene was surreal. She was wearing blue jeans and her "World's Best Grandma" crew neck sweatshirt, which were her favorite clothes and exactly what she had wanted to be dressed in. Her final outfit was topped with a bright, multicolored knit hat she had worn since losing her hair. The hat had been handmade by volunteers at the hospital. A basket in the family room of the oncology wing had been filled with them and replenished every week.

Tyler had made a fleece blanket for his Ama for Christmas. He had made a second one for her in the days leading up to her death that was sized especially for her to take with her in the coffin. The blanket was spread across her lap and legs. I look at my mother's face. As you would expect, it looked like her but not quite. Something still wasn't right, so I examined her closer.

This was a woman who was typically smiling, with teeth showing. She had her mouth shut, and she was somewhat frowny. I realized she had no teeth. All at once, I broke out laughing because I forgot to give the funeral home the dentures. I remembered her blue jeans; I remembered her fancy hat, but I forgot her teeth.

"Are you okay?" asked the funeral attendant.

"We forgot her dentures!" I said.

"We wondered where her teeth were," he said.

"Why didn't you call me?" I asked, laughing very hard. I couldn't remember the last time I had smiled this much. I brought the rest of the family in and told them about the dentures, and we all simply roared.

Laughing just broke the moment wide open. Having the body of my mother lying in a coffin in my grandparents living room was bizarre. I knew it wasn't her any longer. She had no more use of this body, and still she was making us smile and laugh. Her spirit could no longer be contained.

This had been a tumultuous March. March is typically marked with rain. My mother loved the rain, which was the literal "silver lining" in our forced relocation to the slate gray and evergreen Pacific Northwest. Not this March, though. The weather was unseasonably dry and sunny from the day we got her home from the hospital until the day she passed. The birds were out and chirping. While she loved the birds, she may have loved the rain more. A few of us had a good chuckle about it. It must've rained the night before her burial. The ground was soft and wet. I remember the way it felt under my feet during the service: soft, supportive, and nourishing.

As much as I knew in my heart that my mother was in a better place, my kids had a really hard time. The home wake didn't make it easier, I think, because we basically replaced the hospital bed with a coffin. They had never experienced the death of a loved one before, certainly not of someone as close as their Ama. The boys felt responsible to their Ama to be her pallbearers. They helped bring the coffin from the hearse to the gravesite. I was proud of them. I was proud of their fortitude and maturity. Aunt B had the toughest time. Everyone was upset and cried, but she was the most visibly shaken. The sight of the grave upset her, and she didn't want us to put her sister in the ground. She struggled. She was gone, and we were burying her body.

My mom was always an upbeat person, and music was such a big part of our lives and how we expressed ourselves. Maybe part of our love of music was using someone else's words for ones we couldn't find on our own. Maybe part of it was how we used it as a window for joy when we couldn't find that on our own either. My mother loved the song "Happy," by Pharrell Williams. I had a friend bring along a small portable speaker. I just knew we'd need it.

After the pastor said a few words, we set blue carnations on her casket, and I played the song. I had queued it up from a playlist that my mom loved to dance to, a playlist that also included the song "Strokin'" by Clarence Carter that has a line dance to it. My mom loved that dance, but I'm not sure if she'd ever really listened to the words before. They are pretty risqué, and they start right in. I handed my cell phone over to my friend, and said, "Be careful. Turn it off right after this song I don't want the next one to play."

Sure enough, seconds after "Happy" finished, the next song kicks in, and Clarence Carter is talking about "makin' love." My youngest looked up at me, slack-jawed and wild-eyed. "Oh my gosh!" he said, "Does Ama know what those words say?" The moment was funny, and we were smiling yet again.

We threw a blue jeans party celebration of life for her the following week. She hadn't wanted anybody coming in black, she wanted everyone dancing and having a good time in blue jeans and sweatshirts. "You have a party and you celebrate," she said.

The party was important to her, so we spent a lot of time on it. We had picture boards and mementos on display. My mom loved line dancing, so we hired a deejay and contemplated every song. We had her party at our friend Louie's Italian restaurant. He had always been there for us, even holding a fundraiser at his place months earlier to help cover her medical expenses. While the restaurant was normally closed on Sunday, Louie opened for us, had staff come in, and kept everyone fed with pizza and a full salad bar. People came all night: old friends, people she worked with, folks came out of the woodwork for her party.

All told, around four hundred people showed up. Louie's place has a stage for live music and a huge dance floor, which was filled up all night. I can just imagine the smile on my mother's face, watching us all having a good time and celebrating her life.

CHAPTER 9

Tear Down the Walls

Let me tell you about where I live. I live in Washington state, near Seattle. I didn't choose this place, it chose me. I stayed because I love it here. Because of Mother Nature, because of the spirit, because of the people and the community, the mountains and the trees. It has given me exactly what I needed to move toward healing.

An amazing singer and musician, Mary Lambert, is a part of this community, and we're so lucky to have her. I have had the pleasure of seeing her perform several times. A hometown favorite, I have always enjoyed her music. I saw her perform in front of a hundred people or so at a fundraiser for the Q Center across the Sound from Seattle. The room was full of emotion, power, and strength. She was the only performer for the event, and she commanded the room with ease, grace, and confidence. She was just one singer who oscillated back and forth between a grand piano and her acoustic guitar, superbly playing both.

One song especially spoke to me, grabbing my heart, shaking me, and reminding me that I was not alone.

She sang:

"Have you ever seen a stampede of horses? Do you wonder what the hooves look like from underneath? Have you ever tasted the blood from biting your own lips because you couldn't say no loud enough?

I never fought back.

I kept my thighs tight and closed, but once he's inside you, you wish you were the seatbelt, streetlamp, store clerk, a bed of calla lilies- anything but a woman.

In that moment, our eyes glaze over, and they stay that way for years. That's what you've lost."

I closed my eyes, wanting to hear each and every word, trying not to be distracted by the girls on their cell phones in front of me, and just absorbing it. The words and her perspective hit me one by one with their meaning. I wanted to soak it all in. I kept thinking, *Was she there? Had she been there when my father raped me? Every time I would act asleep and throw my arms around hitting him, faking I was asleep? Was she there when I would firmly say 'No! Stop! Don't do this to me ever again!'*

This singer before me was clearly younger than me. I imagined her hiding in the walls of my house because she was describing with such intimacy what this abuse felt like. Of course, she wasn't there in my home. She had her own experience and her own pains: the unfathomable heartache, the familiar depression, and the feeling of being lost. I got the sense she knew all of it. And, there we were: just the two of us. I was sitting cross-legged on the floor, and she was singing and talking directly to me.

Giving voice to your experience is important to me. Since becoming more vocal about my experience as an incest survivor, I meet people all the time who have been abused or raped but haven't talked about it; I mean, even in therapy. I feel they are ashamed of themselves. What I know, and what Mary shared, is that none of us are alone. We all are strong. We are fighters and worthy of survival.

Her words reminded me to continue to fight, to continue to dream, to continue to share because those actions make a difference one little step at a time, each of us a ripple of energy. I want to thank her for helping me remember that our voices matter.

Over the years I learned that survivors of incest or rape are often asked, "What did you say to make them do this to you?"

Classic victim-blaming bullshit, and I can't stand it.

"What were you wearing? What did you say?" As if to ask, "How exactly did you ask for this?"

If you are or were a victim, being attacked or abused is not your fault. Being abused wasn't my fault, and it isn't your fault. A child does not say, do, dress, or behave in any manner that invites a grown adult to engage in terrible acts like sodomy, pedophilia, or any other type of abuse. Period.

Don acted as though I owed him something. Having this grown man treat me like I had done something to deserve all that pain was a very strange feeling. I am still bewildered at the questions or the statements that I hear. Child sexual abuse has such a stigma in our society, speaking of the topic is still rare. I just can't fathom that any adult would even think that a child could ask to be abused in any way, shape, or form.

On January 27, 1994, Don plead guilty to child rape in the first degree.

The man who society called my father but was crueler than the devil was sentenced to an "exceptional sentence" of seventeen years and sent away to the special sexual offenders' prison on McNeil Island.

Sometimes people ask me if I feel like seventeen years was long enough. The truth is that what Don took from us totals up to far longer than seventeen years. Especially for my brother. His whole life has been impacted by this in a way with which he has never been able to deal. I truly believe that much of what has happened in my brother's life is related to the physical, emotional, and sexual abuse that he suffered at the hands of our father.

Although I don't remember any instances of abuse before 1978 (I was four), I learned during this process that Don believed I was born to be his concubine, to curry his sexual favors. My father testified that he had begun sexually abusing me as an infant.

As an infant. He admitted that his first sexual touch of me was when I was a mere ten days old. And if he was doing that to me at such an age, I know damn well he was doing it to Cory too.

So, is a seventeen-year sentence justice?

I'm not even sure I can comprehend the question.

Part of me didn't want him to have the luxury of pleading guilty. I wanted him to stand in front of a jury of his peers and have them say, "No, you're crazy, you did wrong." "Sure, there was a moment where the judge said, "You deserve the worst sentence I can give you." Part of me knows that it doesn't matter who might have said this to him. A hundred people could say that to him, and it's not going to change his perspective on the ways things went."

Don never showed remorse for what he did. He continued to be adamant that he had done nothing wrong, and he was actually kicked out of group therapy for sex offenders by the other offenders themselves for hindering their progress. I don't have any delusions that Don thinks anything differently today than he did back then. We were asking for it, he said.

Looking back now, as sad as it is, we're lucky he got the sentence he did. Now that I'm older, I recognize the prosecutor was probably right. He might not have gotten seventeen years. He might not have gotten even ten, or five, or even one year. Who knows. I saw a case on the news recently where someone got just six months for the rape of a child.

As I look back now I think seventeen years was a decent sentence given the system was entirely created to benefit a man like him, who had top security clearance in the NSA and multiple college degrees. Don was a smart man who fought in wars and served our country. Kids going against a man like that in a trial? Who knows what the outcome would have been.

Just consider jury selection when attorneys ask the jurors if they have ever been victims of this type of crime. When I think of the numbers of women and men who have been victims of sexual abuse, all the #metoo stories, the harassment. Half the women raise their hands and are summarily dismissed, as though this violence disqualifies you from being able to hear the case. I've had it happen to me.

The crime victim's advocate called in 2005 and said Don was getting out after serving only eleven years. My heart sunk, and I started to panic. I could feel myself reliving everything again, except now I had two sons and knew that I had to protect them. I immediately filed for a lifetime restraining order to ensure that neither my children nor I would ever be contacted by him.

Shockingly, Don fought the restraining order. He stated that he wasn't a violent man and that he wouldn't ever hurt us. How this convicted child rapist was going to be released from prison even though he had no remorse and no qualms for what he had done was a travesty to the justice system. And to think of how much pain he was possible of inflicting on others, both physical and emotionally. And, he knew of my children.

The commissioner who oversaw the restraining order hearing was very kind. The court wouldn't transport him, so she asked if we had read his rebuttal, and if there was anything I wanted to add. I simply stated that any human being who would do what he did to children, from infancy and without remorse, is an inherently violent and dangerous person, and I hoped his statement wouldn't alter her opinion. The commissioner said that she agreed with me and honored the restraining order immediately.

I don't know what I thought he was going to do. I didn't think he would hurt me, but it didn't feel like long enough. He wasn't remorseful and I didn't trust him. I believed he would stalk my babies, or me, again after all this time. I wanted him to stay in prison longer. If a seventeen-year sentence felt like an imbalanced compromise, then eleven years, just two-thirds of that, felt like a shock. I was involved in that conversation with local police and Department of Corrections before he was paroled and that's when they told us what had happened.

The state of Washington has a labeling committee that classifies sex offenders into levels one, two, or three, based on offenses and probability of recidivism, with level three being most likely to reoffend. Don had been classified as a level one sex offender. They explained what level one meant. He had been classified as a level one because we were his children, and he had been deemed as nonviolent and least likely to reoffend. We hadn't yet learned that Don sexually abused a cousin of mine in New York. She confessed in a letter to me and later died of asphyxiation during surgery.

I had to introduce my then five-year-old son to his grandfather via pictures of him from the parole board. "This man is a bad man who does bad things to children," I said and pointed to the image of a gray-haired man he had never met. "If you ever see him anywhere you run screaming and find an adult immediately. Do you understand me?"

Jaycob nodded, his blue eyes understanding only my urgency. I explained that this man was my father, and he made bad choices that he could never take back, and the result of those bad choices were that he can never be part of our lives.

I cried more after that conversation than I had all along. What a conversation to have with your five-year-old. As a parent, I never wanted to have that conversation, and I know more of those talks are coming as my children grow up and want to learn more about the grandfather they never knew and I hope they never meet.

Authorities must notify victims of an abuser's release, the address to which he's registered to move to when he gets out, what the abuser looks like, when he will be released, and what he's likely going to look like in six months. I was in a victims' witness protection program for a year, during which I had an emotional relapse and went back to individual counseling. Getting through the trauma of Don's being released was tough, but thanks to a wonderful support network and the help of an amazing therapist I was able to do it.

We've heard to forgive our trespassers or all the pain and anger will eat us alive from the inside. Holding on to hate, they say, is like drinking poison and thinking it's the other person who will suffer. Later, when I finally learned of how Don had abused my cousin, I felt like the hate would never let up. Something had to give. I had to move forward somehow and not let him or his actions control my life. I could no longer stomach that poison.

A therapist at that time worked with me to "forgive" him. I wish I could say I was a true believer in forgiveness. Especially forgiveness for such horrific treatment, but how can a daughter ever forgive her biological father for committing these unspeakable acts? When the time was right, I wrote him a letter as part of my process, my therapy. The words poured from me and at the end, I wrote that I forgave him for what he had done, but I'm not sure I believed it.

This was from a place of wanting to be free and be myself, not forgiving him such that I might develop some type of relationship with him. I had to forgive him so that I could release myself. I wanted to give myself the forgiveness, and to do that, it needed to be real and not be just going through the motions. I prayed and prayed for the strength to knock down those walls that had hardened around my heart. It was an emotional, internal surrender, a turn in my soul and in my spirit. I came to a place where nothing that happened to me was allowed to control my life or drive my thought and emotion. I "forgave" in the outward saying of it so that I could move on.

Even now, as I write this at age forty-four, the daily reminders are there. The flashes, the memories. I can't look in the mirror sometimes. That genetic pollutant that I have no choice against. He was blessed with two children and took liberties with us that no human should ever be allowed to take with a child. Those memories greet me in the mirror every day. It's as real as my own flesh and bone and will never ever go away as long as I live.

Forgiveness, for trauma at this level is a myth. I can't forgive him, but I am no longer standing in perpetual victimhood either. At the beginning I didn't think that I would ever get over the devastation that Don caused. I was suffering a constant hum of anxiety that often grew so loud I wondered if he was driving around and watching me. The stalking of my youth and teenage years left me constantly wondering if I was being followed. The feeling was relentless. I was late to work on several occasions because I had to pull over to let the feeling pass or even get out of my car and look around. Because if he was following me, I wanted to make it known that I was strong and wouldn't be his victim ever again.

I never mailed the "forgiveness" letter. For me the act of writing the letter were enough to make a difference. I could feel the poison of that resentment slowly easing its grip on me. Something I learned during the years of counseling was that I could pack away the memories and at any time I could unpack them, but they didn't have to rule my life. Understanding what that meant and how I could use it took a long time but was pivotal in my healing. Real and true forgiveness is something that you have to do for yourself. Sometimes it is a daily practice.

A spot called Paradise, on Mt. Rainier, is the place I've gotten as close to paradise in my self as I've ever felt. We were up at 5,000 feet elevation, with the sun shining down on the snow creating a beautiful scene. The boys were learning to snowboard, while I looked on and took in nature. I breathed deeply and thought about my past, about the hold that this man still had on my daily life. I steadied myself in the moment, slowed my breathing, and heard the giggles of children in the distance. The moment stood still.

Every breath I took, pulling the cool in, cleansing my lungs, allowed my shoulders to relax and drift away from my ears, shedding years of tension that had been ingrained into my nervous system. I continued to breathe deeply, intentionally, and an ultimate peace fell over my body.

I don't know exactly what the trigger was. I don't know why that moment or where the calm came from, but it washed over me. And from that moment forward I knew I wouldn't be crippled by the thoughts of the past. The snow was crisp, and my children were happy and with me, I was no longer afraid of hell.

Been there, done that.

I finally knew it, and in some way, my ordeal was over. In that moment I realized that I had survived hell. Some ancient internal strength brought me through. I'm not sure from where that strength came. But I survived, and I have now created a haven. I was free, and I *am* free, free to go forward being the best person I can be. On top of that mountain I felt at peace for the first time ever. I will never forget how it felt inside my soul, how my heart was calm, and spirit was free.

Maybe it was God after all. Maybe God couldn't prevent the atrocities but did provide the wellspring of strength that brought me through. The chaos of this world has no reason, no logic. If God exists, and that's where the strength for my survival came from, then

I owe a debt of gratitude, and I will pay it on as many mountaintops and vistas of splendor I can climb and enjoy.

. . .

The devastation of missing my mother surfaces at times I would expect, such as holidays and special events like her grandchild's concert or play. The first anniversary of her death was approaching when one of the boys said: "Ama should be here."

I could hear it emerge from the depths of his own aching heart. I was reminded of all the things she would miss throughout the rest of our lives. The grief cracked me open again. Over and over I am confronted with the same themes: I needed to know more. We all needed to know more. We should have asked more questions. I should have charged ahead and made myself uncomfortable and made better decisions and not suffered as a victim of ignorance and complacency.

My mother didn't know my brother and I were being abused. It's interesting; I think I have learned it generationally. My family has always been the type to want to protect each other, even when it's not the right thing to do. In our protecting, a lot of hurt has happened. A lot of fear and anger and hurt stems from this need to protect. "We don't talk about it." "Nobody needs to know what happens in of our home." I think it's a learned behavior from a very young age.

We didn't know why we were moving to Washington state. My mother didn't get a second opinion when she went to that sham small town doctor in 2000 who basically condoned that she keep smoking like a chimney. I never asked the oncologist about the reality of her prognosis when he said she had stage-four cancer. We didn't know what radiation was going to look or feel like. We didn't get second opinions, and she suffered.

To me all these things beg the question: if we had really known how bad it was at diagnosis, would we have done the same things? Would we have allowed her to pursue an aggressive schedule of chemo and radiation therapies that made her suffer through indescribable pain and burned her throat so badly she couldn't even eat, one of life's simplest pleasures? Or would we have just taken it easy? Eaten delicious things. Spent time at the coast with the boys. Watched the birds poke around in the feeder. How could the last ten months of her life have been different if we hadn't been so hell-bent on her fighting, and instead we had focused on quality of life?

Once my mother entered hospice care, a nurse gave me a sheet of paper spelling out how the next days were going to go. They knew exactly everything that was going to happen, and the speed at which her body was going to change. They even explained what we were going to go through emotionally. But no one warned us what ten months of chemo was really going to look like. No one told us what radiation would do to her neck. Silence is the real perpetrator: death cloaked in sheep's clothing.

We need to make a difference, and we can make a difference. I do believe a power larger than me exists, and one day I hope to ask that power why, not only for myself, but on behalf of the 3.3 million children who are abused each year, and for the five children who die each day in the United States due to abuse. Why are such horrific crimes allowed to happen if such an all-knowing, all-powerful spirit or being truly exists?

I think it's important to stand strong for children and stop the cycle of violence. Part of the challenge is discomfort with the subject, puritanical roots covering our mouths with gags of shame. Let's stop the self-hating cycle of shame and silence that perpetuates this abuse and strips children of their very lives. After all these years, to review those court records and read my youthful handwriting, which has spent two decades relegated to the vault of some bureaucratic filing cabinet in a basement somewhere, was intensely moving. I remembered the feeling within my body when I wrote those words, being honest for the first time after years of hiding.

I've evolved since then. Now I've got clinical words and phrases in my vocabulary from all the work I've done, words like "pedophile" and "sodomy." I was on those pages, my voice young and fresh and raw and aching with abuse, straining against the silence of all those years. That is what's essential and vital for me. I must examine what I have the courage to withstand and learn to break through the glass in my throat to ask questions and speak hard truth.

. . .

My youngest son is an actor. He has an agent who sends him gig opportunities all the time for him to see if he's interested and in submitting an audition. She submitted Tyler for a part in a public service announcement on a local Seattle station regarding child sexual abuse. Talk about hitting home. Not only did it give me an opportunity to talk more about this subject with him, but if he chose to audition for the part, it would be his first PSA, and a great opportunity for him to be a part of something I feel extremely passionate about.

The PSA was about speaking up and prevention and provided a powerful opportunity for me to connect with him about the topic. We were in the car. We have a lot of good conversations in the car. That's when I have the boys alone and can get their undivided attention.

"We got an email today from Melissa," I said, "it's called a PSA." I explained what a PSA is, what it means, and I explained that this PSA was about child abuse. "It's good work," I said, "it's a good thing to draw attention to."

He asked what child abuse meant. I explained abuse and body privacy, and how it's okay to talk about these things. My kids are aware that my father is a bad man, but I'm always sensitive as to what is age appropriate. What they should or shouldn't hear. How much they can take. They're very smart. Most kids are way smarter than they get credit for. My kids will process things on their own over a few weeks and then come back and belt out questions.

"We need to be doing important work," he said, "this sounds like important work, so let's audition for this one."

He may audition for hundreds of parts and not get a call, but he did get this one. I talked about the script with my son and let him read the words. After he filmed it, I explained to him that this is what happened to me and why his grandfather is not involved in our lives. As of the time of this writing, I still haven't broached the sexual component of the abuse because I don't think he's ready for it, but we talked about adults, and how abuse can happen between kids too.

I explained it's important that kids know it's okay to talk about abuse because I didn't know how to talk about when I was a kid, which kept me from telling an adult about what was happening. I was an adult by the time I learned how bad the abuse I suffered was, and it was finally taken care of. And that is unacceptable. The message in the PSA was intense. Nine out of ten abusers are someone who the family and the child know, most of whom are in the inner family circle. Abusers say things like "it's just between us" or "don't tell," or the abuser might threaten punishment.

The abuser perpetuates a grotesque cycle of shame and silence that can only ever be broken with discussion, dialogue, questions, and getting just a little uncomfortable so that the truth can come out.

The topics of child abuse and incest are unspeakable in many ways, but we must talk about it, just like we have to talk about sex with our kids. Are you ashamed of the word? Can you say it in conversation without blushing or worrying about saying it? Have you talked to your children about sex? Have you talked about private areas and why they're private? Have you talked about consent? We never talked about sex in our home while I was growing up. Everything I knew about sex, I knew at a very young age because of the sexual abuse at the hand of my father or because of what I heard at school. We couldn't talk about it at home because it was a bad word, and we all suffered in silence as a result. Being ashamed of our bodies, ashamed of sex, will get us and future generations nowhere. This is a conversation that could mean life or death to children.

Sometimes I wonder if I had spoken up sooner about the abuse, more than just a vague statement about my father loving me differently, had been taught, had been talked to, if things would have been different. Who knows? It might not matter now for me, but there is still an opportunity to help others.

One thing that's important to know is how children often show us rather than tell us that something is upsetting them. Many reasons for changes in a child's behavior exist, but a combination of worrying signs may mean that it is time to call for help or advice.

Here are some signs to watch out for in children:

- Acting out in an inappropriate sexual way with toys or objects
- Nightmares, sleeping problems
- Becoming withdrawn or very clingy
- Becoming unusually secretive
- Sudden unexplained personality changes, mood swings, and insecurities
- Regressing to younger behaviors, like bedwetting
- Unaccountable fear of specific places or people

I wanted to try and always see things like I was looking through the eyes of a child. It's something I never really could do during my own adolescence. I wanted to see through skin color, sexuality, the past, and people's pain. I wanted to always see the good in all things. I promised myself that my children one day would experience and try everything. That they would see through my eyes to capture the passion in the world and the people around them.

As a child my vision was tainted and blurry. The sights ahead of me felt foggy, sad, and miserable. But at that moment when the judge looked at me with pain and tears in his eyes that whispered, "it's going to be okay," I knew it was true. At that moment the world was different. All those people involved: police, my family, judges, lawyers, social workers, and counselors, renewed my sight and gave me vision to a new life and a new hope.

"Look for the helpers," that's what Mister Rogers says. When everything seems to be going wrong, look for the helpers. "You will always find people who are helping."

That day in court I promised myself that my eyes would never blind themselves from the atrocities of the world by becoming foggy and tuning out. I wouldn't miss anything ever again: the beauty of the clouds, the sky, people, or life itself. I never wanted to miss the opportunity to smell a flower, take a picture, or talk to some random person on the street. Sometimes people might wonder why I do some of the things I do. Why I take so many photos or write down quotes. I was so isolated for so long, so afraid to show myself to the world for fear that someone might find out my secrets that now I just want you to be able to see through my eyes. For just a moment to know what life is like in this skin.

This is my crazy life, and it sure as hell has been painful at times, but I survived and now I am enjoying it as much as I can. With every bone in my body, with every ounce of my being, I want to assure all children in my world that they are safe and loved, and get opportunities to experience amazing adventures. I want them to know that they are valuable. They can speak up and have the courage to ask hard and important questions. We all must speak up and ask questions because time is the only thing we've got, and silence is an abdication of power.

To this day, whether when I am deep in the throes of dealing with the never-ending consequences of my own abuse or hearing details about some gruesome case somewhere in the world, I just can't understand what drives a person like Don. My mind cannot even consider wrapping itself around the idea of understanding. But that's what insanity is, right? Completely unexplainable. A sickness.

Sickness begets sickness.

On more than one occasion I have considered suicide to try to escape the mad man who was my biological father. I journaled about how I would do it. I don't know that I could say I was seriously contemplating ending my life, but I know that it crossed my mind more than once. It's quite common. The *British Journal of Psychiatry* published research in July 2008 highlighting what many victims of abuse could tell you, that children who are repeatedly abused or are abused by a member of their immediate family are at higher risk of attempting suicide in later life.

Overall, the study links suicide attempts and childhood abuse and shows that the characteristics of the abuser and the severity of the trauma may be important additional factors of suicide risk. The study found that the risk of suicide in later life is related to the frequency of abuse during childhood and the identity of the abuser. Repeated abuse, according to expert analysis, was more strongly associated with suicide attempts than a single occurrence of abuse, while sexual abuse by an immediate family member, such as a father, stepfather, or brother, carried the greatest suicide risk, far greater than abuse perpetrated by an extended family member or an unrelated individual.

Researchers propose two possible explanations for this pattern: First, abuse by a close family member such as father or brother is considered especially traumatic, not just because of the intimacy of that relationship, but potentially also because such abuse is more likely to occur in families with multiple issues that prevent these families from providing safe and healing conditions following abuse. Second, trauma caused by close family members may have long-term consequences on the development of healthy attachment patterns necessary for mental health. The question of how this type of stress changes a person on a genetic level is also pertinent.

By studying the brains of suicide victims, Patrick McGowan from the Douglas Mental Health University Institute, found that child abuse modifies a gene called NR3C1 that affects a person's ability to deal with stress. The changes it wrought were "epigenetic," meaning that the gene's DNA sequence wasn't altered but its structure was modified to make it less active. These types of changes are long-lasting, which strongly suggests that the trauma of child abuse could be permanently inscribed onto a person's genes.

Finally, consider the pain of Bill Zeller, a 27-year-old Princeton Ph.D. candidate and renowned internet programmer. Zeller stunned the programming community with a 4,000-word suicide note detailing a childhood filled with physical and sexual abuse. According to the *Daily Princetonian*, Zeller posted the note on his website and emailed it to friends before taking his own life. He had never disclosed his abuse to anyone. He requested the note be reprinted only in its entirety, so I will respect those wishes. Just search Google for "Bill Zeller suicide note," and you'll see the whole thing, often followed by dozens, even hundreds of comments depending on the site, where people bare details of their own abuse and suicidal ideation.

I thought about it, taking what people call "the easy way out" after everything had been so hard and traumatizing. A permanent solution to a problem that seemed equally unending, but I couldn't leave my mother like that. For myself, I considered suicide a selfish act, though it was sure to end the pain, tears, and fear. I could see the appeal.

I journaled and fantasized about it, but did not take steps to realize these ideas. For years it would be like something that I could touch, something I could lean on when things got too crazy. I had a way out; I could touch the edge of the pool when things got too turbulent in my mind. I wondered about pills, about blades and bathtubs, about plummeting off a bridge to murky doom, anything to make it stop. Suicide represented a perverse kind of safety net that I could use to make everything disappear if I really wanted. Thank God, I held on. It's amazing what we have the courage to withstand.

• • •

When Don got out of prison, he went to live with someone, supposedly an aunt, but it was so strange that none of us knew he had a family member who lived in Washington state before then. After he was released I decided to drive my yellow Beetle to the location provided by the crime victim's advocate and confront him. I had so much to say. I wanted him to know the damage that he had caused, the devastation to my mother and how my brother continued to suffer long after the abuse had ended. I wanted to scream and yell at him for telling the prosecutors that my young brother asked to be raped and deserved everything he got.

Mostly I wanted him to know that he couldn't break me. I wanted him to see that I had survived despite what he had done to me and the unending impact of those choices. His comments about my weight or my looks didn't break me. I wanted him to know that the horrific things that he did to me from infancy through my teenage years weren't going to control my life forever. I wanted him to feel my anger, but I also wanted him to see that I had made it, that I was good, and I that was going to make something of myself one day.

In the statement he made when I filed the lifetime restraining order, he referenced his excitement that I had children, that being a grandfather was always his dream, and that he had hoped that he could be a part of lives. This bastard probably wrote with the intention of trying to make his way back into my life. I wanted him to know that the moment he started raping me was the day he lost the right to be a father or a grandfather. I wanted him to know what he could never have.

I pulled up to the address on the victim's protection notification of release, but was careful not to pull into the driveway. As I was getting up the gumption to get out of my car, the main door opened and he stood behind the glass of the storm door.

My heart pounded within my chest. I felt a knot in my throat. His evil eyes locked on me immediately with the exact same courtroom stare he had during his sentencing. I will never forget that look. His hair had gone almost fully white, and he was heavier than he had been eleven years earlier. He stood with his hand on the door handle, his lips pursed like always.

When I saw him, the rage flamed up, but the scared child inside me did as well. I could hear his voice in my head, telling me everything that I wouldn't ever be. I could hear him blaming me for his failed marriage with my mother. The voice in my head was so loud and clear, it was as if he were standing in front of me saying it all, right at that moment. I started my car after a few of the longest moments of my life, looped around the cul-de-sac, and paused to look at him one more time, then I drove off. I realized on the drive back that he still had control and that my mission was going to be to break that reign he had over my life and move on. I left there on a mission to make change for myself and other survivors.

In late 2016, I met with a reporter from KOMO news, an ABC affiliate out of Seattle. In the years after the criminal sentencing, Cory and I had filed and won a civil suit to try and recoup damages for the years of abuse. Don was in jail at the time. My case was thrown out due to the statute of limitations, but Cory won a $5 million settlement. This amount would have readily subsidized therapy and counseling that we both desperately needed. Given that he was in jail at the time of the civil suit, Don had no income. However, he stood to receive his military pension following release.

Then the bomb dropped: because of a legal technicality his military pension could not be garnished. Not a penny of the $5 million settlement against this abuser could be paid to his victims, his children, because his retirement happened to be from the U.S. military. The Uniformed Services Former Spouses' Protection Act (USFSPA), 10 USC § 1408 states that military retirees are not subject to garnishment, except in the case of child support, spousal support, or property division. No exceptions are provided.

That's when I began the journey of writing letter after letter to everyone I could think to try and call attention to this matter, and get the law changed. My senators, representative, governor, local legislators, and news outlets, editors, and lawyers. After twenty-two years of writing, calling, and emailing I made one final plea via email to a few local news stations. The judgment was set to expire the following month, and this was my last-ditch effort to get any attention.

Finally, I received a call from an investigative reporter for KOMO. Soon I was wedged in a small room at their broadcast studio staring down the barrel of a huge, professional television camera.

"Do you think someone is preventing that law from being changed on purpose?" asked the reporter.

I don't remember now what I said. I went blank, fogged out on stress-induced autopilot just as I had fought to shake off all those years ago. What I hope to learn to articulate someday is that I think in our society, those who serve in the military are deemed heroic although many aren't heroes. Many sit behind desks and push paper, necessary work, sure, but let's not conflate that with heroism.

Don served nineteen years and eight months. Two months shy of the twenty years of active service that triggers your spouse to automatically get half of the retirement benefits. Cunning, manipulative Don retired just short of that timeframe so that my mom didn't get full retirement benefits as his spouse.

Multiple psychologists have said that everything he did was an intentional act. Everything.

My mother got some spousal benefits, but not what she was entitled to, especially for all she endured at his hands. When she died, everything returned to him. He's back to collecting full benefits, which at an officer's wage is surely not peanuts.

In January 2017, more than two decades after we won the lawsuit, I met with my Representative to Congress, Suzan DelBene. She learned about my story from the news story, and she wanted to close the gap in the law. She asked legislative staff to prepare a bill to introduce when the new session began. That bill has passed, and was signed into law on December 12, 2017, closing this one loophole, although the Department of Defense negotiated for a cap the offender's garnishment restitution at 25%. Why? It makes you wonder if something is in place to purposefully protect someone, *or someone's*, in high places. This fight is not over for me, but I can smile at the victory of one battle more than two decades in the making. One battle in a long war with far too many innocent victims.

Anyone who abuses a child doesn't deserve to be treated like a hero. Even in this highly charged political climate: I don't care if that person was on the front lines of Vietnam or was a decorated Marine. Inflicting pain and suffering on a defenseless child is not heroic, but I think our society makes defaulting to heroism around military regardless of merit an act of political correctness. We stand, we clap, and while I agree that freedom isn't free, I've been victimized by a man of the flag, and I know his so-called allegiance to it doesn't make him a better person. A man like that is a disgrace to his uniform.

I think it's true that in a jury trial these facts would have been stacked up against us. Looking back, I don't think he would have gotten an exceptional sentence if it were trial by a jury. We might have ended up with child rape in the third degree, punishment for which is in-home treatment or something ridiculous like that. The reality is that prison sentences end. He spent eleven of seventeen years, got out, and had military retirement stockpiling that whole time he was in prison, and he now continues to receive pay.

Don remarried and owns properties and businesses registered in his wife's name, as well as access to her grandchildren and a demonstrated mindset that he had done nothing wrong. This man raped, molested, and emotionally abused us our entire lives. He physically beat my brother. He manipulated us all, and after all that, he's considered a level one sex offender, gets out of prison six years early, and had to be registered as a sex offender for only one year. That's right: one year.

Because of our system, the chances that anyone could learn this information about him is slim to nonexistent. The best chance would be if someone went to Pierce County District Court and specifically searched his name, and went back far enough. Don is not on any offender list or any other list anyone would be worried about. He's living a normal life when he should not be able to live near a school, a playground, or have access to anyone's grandchildren.

He served time, lost eleven years of his life, but compare that to my brother Cory. My tortured brother, who battles to function every single day. In the end, has justice been served? Was eleven years served in these circumstances restitution for Cory's past forty years of hell? Everyone who lives within a mile of Don, at least, should know what he's done. The sad part is that I know cycles of abuse are generational. I know it on paper, but it showed itself to me while I was giving a workshop recently.

I listened to one of the attendees speak of her abuse, and her story just went around and around. It's often on the same cycle as poverty, but not always. Whatever the origin, abuse to this degree of intimacy is perpetrated in a cycle that must be interrupted to be broken for good.

I think part of Don's deal, and why I have to try and forgive him to save myself, is that his mom was physically abusive toward him. She called him worthless, no better than his father, and beat him with a baseball bat, I'm told. In talking with family, I've also learned accounts of at least two people raping him as a boy. I am thankful that between my brother and me, in our level, the cycle seems to have stopped. Yes, Cory has made some bad choices, and he's paying his consequences, but he's never physically hurt anybody. He's never sexually assaulted anybody. As damaged as he is, I am hopeful that on some level this has stopped with us, because for so many other victims of abuse it recurs generation after generation.

I feel bad for the people who can't break out of that cycle and get to something different. That's how I feel about my brother. He is currently serving time for a nonviolent crime. When he is done with this sentence, I want to help him to get into intensive therapy. It will be a lot of work, but it will be the only chance he has at a life he deserves or even some inner peace.

• • •

Have you ever wondered how you will be remembered? If you had the chance, would you ask someone how they remember you?

It wasn't until my mother was in the hospital that I thought about legacy. Through the journey at the end of my mother's life, she and I discussed this question. We talked about what her life and her cancer journey might mean for others.

I thought about generational cycles. My grandmother had high expectations, expectations that made my mother more passive, and she married Don and continued to be passive. Finally, toward the end of her life, she broke out and was more assertive than she ever had been. My mother bore the brunt of the perfection of a first child, where with my aunt the pendulum swung in the opposite direction. My grandmother would pine: "She never did anything wrong! Why was it she who got the cancer?"

Both my mom and aunt were smokers. Such a horrible addiction and, like many addictions, terribly hard to quit. Both lived lives centered on caring for children, but my mother was the kind of care taker who would have loved to spend all of her spare time rescuing any kind of animal in need. My mother loved to rescue puppies that had been abused and needed love. She had a knack for bringing them back and giving them a great life. She loved her children and grandchildren with all her heart. She would do anything for us, and she treasured every minute with us. She was there when her grandsons were born, and she watched them grow from wee little things until now. She always wanted them to see the beauty she saw in people and in nature. They loved her tremendously and she loved them even more.

I had the opportunity to see my mother through the eyes of our great-aunts, her career coworkers, and her friends over the last weeks of her life. Everyone agreed that she was kind, sweet, caring, hard-nosed, and hardworking. She was a wonderful mother and an amazing friend.

My mother left a legacy of memories of her goodness and kindness. Those were the things my mother strived for, and those were the things people talked about. My mother was excellent at cheering up people, doing for others, and having a good time. She was dedicated and committed and always put others before herself.

I started the ritual of journaling nightly after she and I discussed this cancer journey. She said, "I hope this is happening so that I may help someone else." Even as the end was nearing it, she did not pity herself, rather it was my mother's wish and my wish to help, someone somewhere else, who one day might have to go through something similar.

No handbook or user manuals are available for anything that is important in this life, for understanding a lover's body, or how to give birth, or how to deal with the end of a parent's life. No manual explains how to emotionally survive abuse, incest, rape, or heal from post-traumatic stress disorder.

Most of us on this planet won't be remembered a hundred years past our demise, but we can leave our imprints here. We leave fingerprints all over this earth and each other, whether we understand this fact or not. The time continues to tick-tock away, yet that impact can echo well past a hundred years. Ask yourself what your legacy will be.

CHAPTER 10

Be the Change

I have seen seven therapists over the past two decades. The first was a state-mandated social worker who I saw weekly. She wanted me to hold and caress my inner child and tell her that I believed that everything would be okay. The idea of holding my inner child just didn't make sense to me, and she didn't explain the reasoning behind the approach and its potential benefits. Frankly, therapy with her felt strange and weird and freaked me out. I told her that I couldn't do it, and I left without finishing the session.

Not surprisingly, I had been having anxiety and night terrors for years. Nights, ever restless, would find me flailing, screaming, kicking, and fighting in my sleep. I had constant panic attacks while driving, fearful I was being watched. I hid it well and no one knew, but I missed work and disassociated from others. I dealt with the anxiety and night terrors, but it was exhausting. I only wanted to sleep. After eighteen years of nearly nightly visits and being treated like a sex toy, my body refused to enter the restful state I needed.

After several years and more therapists, I found one who suggested eye movement desensitization and reprocessing (EMDR) therapy, which is an integrative psychotherapy approach that uses a set of standardized protocols incorporating elements from many different approaches to treat trauma. Scientific research has established EMDR as effective treatment for post-traumatic stress disorder as well as panic attacks, phobias, dissociative and personality disorders, addictions, sexual or physical abuse, body dysmorphic disorders, and disturbing memories.

I had high hopes in the days leading up to the appointment. I wasn't expecting a miracle, but my mind was buzzing with the idea that this process could relieve me of the unending anxiety, panic attacks, and night terrors. I drove to the appointment in silence. Unlike previous visits, the waiting room was empty except for the water cooler, small water fountain, and the soothing sounds of nature music, and me. I looked suspiciously at the magazines scattered about the lobby, took a deep breath, and waited. The therapist's office was dimly lit. Two chairs faced each other but were offset so that they were not directly across from each other.

The therapist told me that I may feel drained and exhausted after the session. Some patients feel the need to sleep for some time afterwards.

Therapy started with his instructions, "Start as far back as you can remember and tell me everything." He had me travel through the timeline of my life like I was sitting on a train and watching my life go by. I narrated what I saw out the window, step by step, phase by phase.

Just as the therapist had predicted, I was completely exhausted after the session. I shut down for a couple of days, not even able to go to work. But sleep came, the best sleep I had ever had

Through that process, and a great deal of self-searching through photography and writing, I got to a point where I could tap into bits and pieces of those memories at my own will. Those blurred, smeared images, which usually sharpened into knife-like focus to torment me without my permission, were accessible if I wanted to retrieve them from my mind, but they weren't constantly invading my everyday moments.

The constant state of anxiety from fear that Don was stalking me lessened. A few days later I drove for the first time without a panic attack. With that I knew it was finally gone. I didn't feel it all rushing in to overwhelm me. I could breathe instead of feeling a weight press on my chest. Instead of stealing my joy, I stood up and conjured my own power back from that limitless well inside of myself. This was a miracle.

I went back a few more times and throughout the years as other things came up. The therapy took a different turn then, becoming more situational. The subject matter shifted from the acts of abuse to the responses ingrained in my brain and body as defense mechanisms. For example, we discussed how my need to please people took a toll on finances or how to understand the difference between holding something in confidence and keeping a secret. I would end up going back just to talk things through, or work on issues that reappeared.

And they always do reappear. In 2005 I was filing restraining orders and meeting with the Department of Corrections regarding Don's release and sex offender level status. I had to take some time off from work, partly for the meetings and hearings, but partly because I was struggling. Although most of the time I kept things hidden, I would sometimes discuss the situation with a coworker. One day she asked, in a sort of off-hand way, why is was such a big deal. After all I had been a little girl when it happened, and he had done his time.

It was time to get over it, she said.

I was angry. I pulled into myself as I usually do. Because of her response, I knew that this coworker had never endured a major trauma. She had no understanding or empathy. The anger swept over me, and I confronted her. I was very direct and told her how abuse as a child can impact someone every day for the rest of their lives. Stories like these are unfathomable to most and not something a person just gets over.

Scars are not just visible, physical things. They can be a profound grief that continually rears its head with any life event, whether when you have kids or get married or a parent dies or you have a consensual sexual encounter.

Maybe over time the abuse gets smaller as it recedes in the rearview, but it's always there just below the surface, and the feeling of loss comes in waves. It dictates how a person learns to live life, who to trust, or feeling the need to keep secrets to protect people. These kinds of things are part of everyday life and cause more damage. Breaking free of that takes a long time and a lot of sunlight in the darkest places.

• • •

I met with my Girl Scout leader from my high school years to tell her what happened and discuss how we can help leaders see signs and recognize clues of abuse. She was devastated and wondered how she could have not noticed. I constantly think about who is going to hear my story and how they will react. I never knew if it was the right time, but as the years went on, I got to a point where every now and then, I would bring up the abuse in some social situation. I offered disclaimers about what I am going to say and asked how much the person with whom I was speaking really wanted to know before proceeding deeper into different aspects of what happened.

As I started to share my story more often like this, I realized that most genuinely listen and acknowledge my experiences. People would say things like, "Oh my gosh, I've never told anybody about my grandfather" or, "I've never told anybody about my dad." Sometimes they'd take a deep breath and tell me their story. Sometimes they'd just give me that knowing look.

"I've just been waiting for him to die," one woman said.

That was when I realized that by telling my truth I could make an impact and help others. I realized that as horrific as my story is, if this is what it does for people, if it allows people to open up and find their voices, then I needed to speak my truth. No longer would I have a noose around my neck just from what he did to me. I began to see that I belonged in the world. That my true self is okay and worth it.

Authenticity is a challenge. How do you know who your true self is when you've been conditioned as I was? When you've endured the kind of physical trauma that my body experienced and when you've seen the things I saw? How do I reclaim myself? Even at forty-four it's hard to know who I really am, and who I am now that I'm on the other side of this story. I am a work in progress and every day I get closer to being truly healed.

I've been seeking my own authenticity for years, going through the motions, unsure if those motions were pointing me in the right direction. I sought out clues by trying to notice when I felt true joy as opposed to the satisfaction that comes with the duty of pleasing other people.

That's why the moment on Paradise at Mt. Rainier stands out so vividly to me. I could feel it as a sensation in my body. I've tried to make that feeling a compass in myself. I've created this path back to myself brick by brick, it's become my foundation.

I have a fire inside of me to prevent other people from having to live through what I've experienced. I know that many children have been through worse, so I started becoming more vocal about exposing my own truth. I converted my writing for therapy into blogging and began sharing news stories, and I started to get comments and emails from other people sharing their experiences and how they never had discussed it with anyone. I was inspired by people who were starting to find their voices after abuse. I started talking to as many people as often as I could.

I worked on special speaking engagements for a local non-profit organization that was putting together a child abuse awareness rally in Washington, D.C. I had my trip planned and my speech written and right before the trip the organization backed out. Since the tickets were already booked, I went and met with senators from Washington to discuss the opportunities available to make changes and help protect children. The experience was powerful, even though many of the conversations were with aides, discussing the topic with my representatives' office made me feel that maybe we would be able to help make a difference.

I had been to D.C. many times during my childhood and was always in awe of the monuments; the pillars on the mammoth-sized buildings. All the power that seemed to live there was amazing. To drive around as an adult and realize that people would hear me and listen inspired me to push for change, to not give up.

I stood in front. I was eight the last time I'd been there. I remember walking up the steps of the Lincoln Memorial. I had just learned about Dr. Martin Luther King Jr. at the time, and I had wondered what step he might have occupied when he gave his famous "I Have a Dream" speech at the greatest demonstration for freedom in the history of our nation.

I wish I had a picture of myself back then and another of this moment. I wanted to see these versions of myself side by side. The moment felt deeply powerful, especially when you consider that Lincoln stands for emancipation and freedom. He's the one who said, "A house divided against itself cannot stand," and I know the truth of that in many ways. Later that day I went to the Martin Luther King, Jr. National Memorial, newly opened for visitors. I think of those two men sometimes, how connected they are, though generations apart. How brave both were to voice unpopular truths to power.

What is bravery? I think it means someone who is courageous and continues moving forward in what they are doing even if they are scared. I have never considered myself brave. I went through life doing what was expected of me to protect those around me. I always thought brave meant stopping Don or standing up and speaking out, but I know now that I did everything I could have done when I was a child.

And what is bravery but doing the right thing even at the risk of suffering? I think maybe it evolves throughout our lives. I was brave to take on suffering as a child to save Cory and my mother. Today, at forty-four, bravery looks like writing this book and splaying open parts of myself again to share uncomfortable details that no one wants to hear, but people need to know. And yes, even still for me this fluctuates. I get powerful moments and then moments when I feel weak. I am exhausted seeing day-after-day news stories of another child who has been hurt. But ultimately, I want to use my voice to help others find theirs and to fix things that are broken, so I ride it out and move forward.

Brave is standing up and finding your voice, even it if shakes. Brave is being kind and helping people even when the world is a scary place. Brave is trying to show up as your best self and share yourself with the world even when you know you're not perfect. Don't be embarrassed or hidden because of your stories. This took me a long time. I didn't want anyone to know what was going on at home, who Don was, or that he was prosecuted. Once I realized that a community was willing to lift me up, everything changed. I am convinced now that "other people's children" don't exist. We all belong to each other.

Find the way the compass in your belly feels when it's pointed at your truth, and then form an undying love for that feeling. It's vitally important. Feel it, believe it, speak it.

• • •

I was working as a delivery driver for the Flying Dutchman Floral Company in the fall of 1993 when Don was out on bond and living in an apartment in Fife, Washington. I happened to be in the shop when my coworker told me there was a call for me. I felt alarmed because no one ever called me at work. I lifted the receiver to my ear.

"Hello," he said, "it's Dad."

I was silent.

"You know, I could go away a long time if you tell them things."

I stood motionless in the cold floral warehouse.

"Okay," I said.

He started to cry and plead, asking me to not tell anyone the details. Prison would be terrible, he said, and it would be a long time before I would be able to see him again. I knew even then it would never be long enough.

"Okay," I said, feet still frozen in place.

"Please," Don begged, "don't ever write a book about me and all of this, don't ever do it."

I was silent. He became irate and repeated himself. "Don't do it, Pennie. Don't you tell them a goddamn thing." His voice coiled like a serpent.

"I have to work now," I said coolly and hung up. That is one of my first courageous moments. A moment I knew the balance of power had begun to shift, and I never forgot it.

Dear Don:

To the man who was part of my inception, but also stole my virginity. To the abuser who caused more hurts than he ever consoled. The man who caused me to sleep with one eye open and be afraid of the dark. To the man who made me take ownership of everyone's lives, causing me to care at a level that I was willing to sacrifice my body:

You need to know that you did not break me. That although there were times of great strife and breaking points, I overcame.

Know that this young girl is no longer afraid of you or your actions. That I have overcome, that I have gained attention at levels you will never see. That my name and the word "survivor" was spoken on the United States Senate Floor as the Child Abuse Accountability Enhancement Act was introduced as a bill to help change things for children after me. That bill now was signed into law on December 12, 2017.

Don, you need to know that I didn't give up. Twenty-two years of writing, calling, and speaking to everyone I could think of. You need to know that my time has finally come, and this momentum is not going to stop. The world is going to know all the horrific things that you have done.

You need to know that I am going to say your name and show your picture, and I am going continue to fight to stop people like you. You are a pedophile, a rapist, a molester, a manipulator, and a criminal, and I have won.

Don, know you didn't break me. I am stronger than I have ever been. I fight daily to assure that people know their value and their worth. I fight to assure that other victims of child abuse find their voices and are able to put monsters like you away. I will never forget the day I asked the judge to have no mercy on you.

I am no longer the small quiet child of whom you took advantage. You have no power over me.

You lost. I won, and I will continue to win.

I am more than a survivor. I am a warrior, and I am larger than life.

-Pennie

PHOTO GALLERY

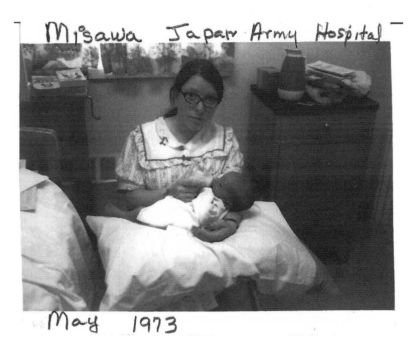

My first portrait. It would be years 18 years before I'd be safe again.

(Photo 1973)

Donald Delosh. Budding photographer and pedophile

1975

Meeting Cory. 1977

I never liked being forced to give hugs or sit on laps. 1978.

Easter, 1979.

Pose. 1981.

Little plastic smiles. 1981.

Portrait of a happy family, 1983.

I was a goalie. Ever vigilent. Always on defense.

Germany, 1985.

Church – Acolytes and Bell Choir

1986

Washington state, 1989.

Still being raped by my father.

"Fishing."

1990.

Class of 1991.
Raped the night before my high school graduation.

The little yellow rambler.

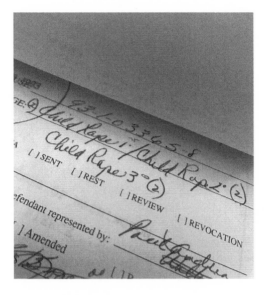

Don was charged with two counts each of Child Rape
in the First, Second, and Third degrees.

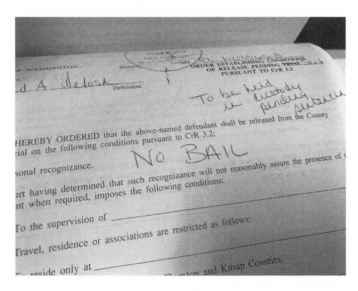

Bail Denied.

Documented evidence of the peep holes.

GERMAN BAKERY TO GET SOME BREAD AND STUFF. HE TOLD ME TO GO DOWNSTAIRS AND HE SAID REAL QUICK. HAD ME LEAN AGAINST THE WALL AND HE PERFORMED ANAL SEX ON ME, IT HURT - I SAID IT HURT TO HIM HE SAID WELL I'M NO BIGGER THEN WHAT COMES OUT OF YOU SO IT CANT HURT.
THERE WERE SEVERAL TIMES HE WOKE ME UP IN THE NIGHT TO GO DOWNSTAIRS AND DO THE SAME THING. AND GO ON ABOUT THE DIVORCE OVER AND OVER, 3 OR 4 times A week And WHEN MY MOM WAS GONE. ALSO WE OWNED A LARGE DODGE RAM VAN AT THE TIME. HED PICK ME UP EARLY FROM SOFTBALL OR SOCCER OR GIRL SCOUTS OR YOUTH GROUP OR HE'D TELL MY MOM WE RAN LATE. ANYHOW THERE WAS A PARK W/ A LARGE PARKING LOT IN IT A COUPLE STREETS BEHIND MY HOUSE. HE'D PARK THE VAN THERE PUT THE SEATS DOWN AND MAKE ME HAVE INTERCOURSE WITH HIM OR ANAL SE IT GOT TO THE POINT WHERE IT WAS HAPPENING ALL THE TIME. THEN WE MOVED ON BASE IN LUDWIGSBURG THINGS WERE STILL GOING ON. HED SAY WE HAVE TO GO UPSTAIRS TO THE

... BECAUSE MY MOTHER HAD SURGERY (A CYST REMOVED ON HER OVARY) THAT SHE COULDN'T HAVE SEX OTHERWISE SHE'D BLEED TO DEATH. SO HE CONVINCED MY BROTHER & I THAT SHE COULDN'T HAVE SEX SO WE'D FEEL SORRY FOR HIM.
I NEVER KNEW ABOUT MY BROTHER, AND MY BROTHER KNEW ABOUT ME. STRANGE BUT TRUE.
I WOULD GO TO BED AT NIGHT AND CRY MYSELF TO SLEEP AND BEGGED TO FORGIVE ME, BUT I FINALLY REALIZED THAT ITS NOT MY FAULT. THEN I WOULD PRAY FOR GOD TO TAKE HIM DURING HIGH SCHOOL I DIDN'T WANT TO COME HOME. I WAS IN SCHOOL ACTIVITIES, AND SPORTS, AND

Investigators had me handwrite my accounts for hours.

Pierce County District Court. Courtroom 127

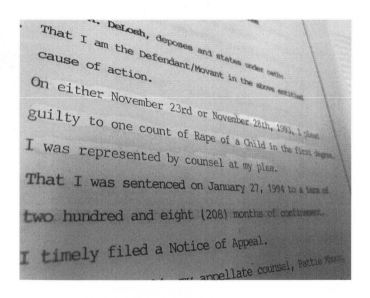

Don pleads guilty to one count of Rape of a Child in the first degree
and was sentenced to 208 months in prison. I'm still not sure
what would have happened if we went all the way to trial.

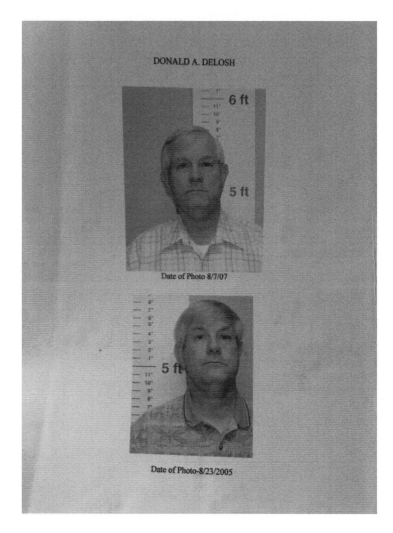

These are the photos that the victims advocate showed me of Don upon his release. These photos are how I introduced my sons to the man who would never be their grandfather.

I will fight with every breath to empower victims against evil like I've known.

The day my mom found the lumps on her neck. I knew that things would never be the same.

The beginning of my mom's cancer fight.

Radiation taking its toll.

Ama and Tyler, November 2013

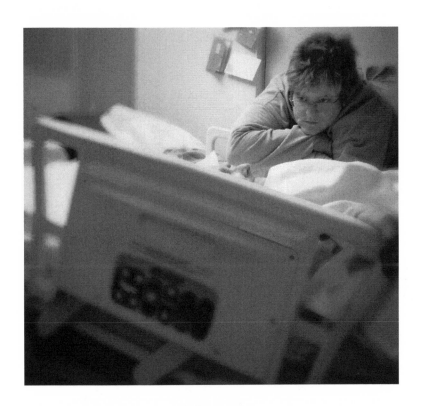

Taking it all in.

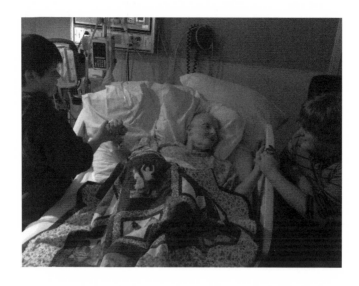

The boys with my mom, "Ama", spending as much time as possible.

Thanks, Mom. Love you.

ACKNOWLEDGEMENTS

Wow. Here we are. Finalized and finally on paper. We made it. I told you story after story, detail after detail, and more. You took all of that and found the most amazing way to present it all. Cat, through the tears and jeers, hours of read-throughs, Skype calls, emails, text messages and random musing; without you, it wouldn't have been possible. Thank you doesn't seem to be enough. Thanks for sticking through – all the way to the beginning! Amazon!

This memoir took years of writing, but also years of living. Special thanks and love to Aaron, Jaycob, Tyler... for understanding, supporting and making space for me and this project.

Erin, Lisa, Kathy, Sarah - editing, reviews, cover, conversations, love and support beyond measure. Thank you!

Anonymous – you helped make this dream come true. Not enough words to thank you.

To my brother, for being brave – so very brave, thank you for breaking the silence. xo

There came a time when being quiet and hidden was no longer an option.

We have only just begun.

xoxo

Pennie